CONTENTMENT HERE AND NOW

A SECULAR BUDDHIST SPIRITUALITY

With thanks to David, the healer, whose art combines competence and compassion.

Dennis Oliver

Edited by Brian Duffy

Illustrated with Buddhist art from past centuries and contemporary reflections by Ian Noble

capercailliecomms.com

Version 1.0

Copyright©2024
Dennis M. Oliver
All rights reserved.

ISBN **979-8-89965-198-4**

Assertion of Author's Rights

Dennis M. Oliver, the author, asserts his exclusive rights to this book. However, you are welcome to print brief quotes from this text, crediting the author. Reprinting extracts excerpts or the diagrams in this book are copyright of the author and are to be used with permission only.

The pictures for Reflection preceding every chapter and the picture on the front cover are original photographs by Ian Noble and require permission for their use. Ian may be contacted through the author.

 The Buddhist illustrations with a few exceptions, are licensed by Wikimedia Commons and are freely available on the Internet.

Dedication

This book is dedicated with grateful memories to my parents, Dr Robert T. Oliver and Mary L. Oliver. They would have approved of me writing the book. Neither were Buddhists, but both strikingly modelled many of the essential perspectives contained in the Buddha's teachings. Both contributed greatly to my appreciation of some of the values and understandings that I have come to value in Buddhism. These include kindness and compassion (from my mother), open-mindfulness and curiosity (from my father), and autonomy and focused effort (from both).

"In every age, men [and women] have set out on pilgrimages, spiritual journeys, and personal quests. Driven by pain, drawn by longing, lifted by hope, singly and in groups, they come seeking relief, enlightenment, peace, power, joy, or they know not what."
Sheldon B. Kopp, *If You Meet the Buddha on the Road, Kill Him! 1976*, Bantam Books

"It seems to me that the most exciting and most revolutionary contribution we can make is to envision and cultivate a contemporary religious sensibility grounded in the long non-theistic tradition of Buddhist thinking and praxis that is entirely in accord with the forms of suffering and the possibilities for awakening now becoming available in our time."
Dale S. Wright, "A Philosophical Assessment of Secular Buddhism", *Insight Journal*, 2015; Barre Centre for Buddhist Studies

"If you want to awaken all of humanity, then awaken all of yourself, if you want to eliminate the suffering in the world, then eliminate all that is negative in yourself. Truly, the greatest gift you have to give is that of your own self-transformation."
Ascribed to Lao Tzu[1], Sixth Century BCE

Stone Buddha Head in Tree Roots[2]

Table of Contents

Letter to a Friend 1
Preface 3
Acknowledgements 8
Map of the Buddha's India, 500 BCE 10
Prelude 13
"This Stuff Really Works!" 13
Retain Your Individuality 15
Make His Teachings Your Own 16
Do What is Helpful for You 17
A Positive Basis for Change 18
Open to Other Helpful Models 18
A Certain Smile 20
Over to You! 21
1. Everything Was Not Enough 25
The Man Behind the Myth 25
A Miracle Child! 27
A Pampered Youth 29
The Legend of the Four Sights 30
Going Forth (The Great Renunciation) 33
Six Long Years of Searching 35
Sujata's Life-Giving Gift 36
Over to You! 38
2. Forty-five Years of Being Buddha 41

His Great Awakening 41
"I am Awake" 43
Making Sense of It All 44
The First Disciples Were Laity 45
The Growing Movement 46
A Master Teacher 46
His Last Months on Earth 50
After His Death 54
Over to You! 56

3. Gotama's Middle Way (*majjhimapatipada*) 59
Universal Truths to Live By 60
A Complex Simplicity 60
Some Will Understand 62
Avoiding Extremes 62
The Benefits of Middle Way Thinking 64
An Ennobling Eightfold Path 65
A Medical Model 67
A Suitable Recovery 68
Over to You! 69

4. Gotama's Twelve-Step Programme 73
The Four Ennobling Realities (*cattāri ariyasaccāni*) 74
Reality #1: We Begin with Our Need 75
Reality #2: The Cause of All Unnecessary Pain 76
Reality #3: Reason to be Hopeful - Suffering is Optional ... 77
Reality #4: A Concrete Way Forward 80
An Example of Eliminating Unnecessary Suffering 80

Four Tasks 81
Twelve-Steps 82
Good News for All Who Live It 85
Over to You! 87

5. Appropriate Perspective *(samma ditthi)* 91
What's 'Appropriate'? 92
Wisdom 92
Soi Sage! 93
Understanding Causation 95
Indra's Net 98
Realistic Uncertainty, Calculated Positivity 99
The Deathless 101
Three Characteristics of Existence 102
Spiritual Evolution 104
Ineffability 107
Over to You! 107

6. Appropriate Resolve *(samma sankappa)* 111
Commitment is Essential 112
A Broader, Deeper Aim 113
From Perspective to Resolve 114
More than Reason 114
Resolving to End Suffering! 115
We Can Love Everyone 116
Practical Application 117
Moving On from Self-Centeredness 118
Progression is Gradual 119

A Hierarchy of Needs and Satisfactions 120
Over to You! 122

7. Ethics: Appropriate Speech, Action, Vocation 125
An Ethical Practice 126
Broad Principles, Not Rigid Rules 127
The Third Aspect: Appropriate Speech (*samma vaca*) 129
The Fourth aspect: Appropriate Action (*samma kammanta*) 132
The Fifth Aspect: Appropriate Vocation (*samma ajiva*) 135
Some Dangers on the Way 137
Keep Moving Forward 139
Over to You! 140

8. Appropriate Effort (*samma vayama*) 143
Mind-Training 144
What Do We Mean by Mind? 145
A Comprehensive, Persistent Effort is Needed 146
Unnecessary Discouragement 147
Persistence 148
The Illusion of Perfection 149
Four Crucial Efforts (*sammappadhana*) 151
The Enemies of Awakening 153
Effort Isn't Everything 156
Authenticity is Required 157
Open to the Unexpected 157
Over to You! 159

9. Appropriate Mindfulness (*samma sati*) 163

What Mindfulness Can Bring to Our Lives 164
The Modern Mindfulness Movement 165
Nine Positive Insights 167
Buddhist Mindfulness 168
Transformation 169
A Developmental Journey 170
A Personal Example 171
Over to You! 172

10. Appropriate Concentration (*samma samadhi*) 175
A Special Kind of Consciousness 176
Flow 178
Levels of Consciousness 179
An Integrated Consciousness 181
Over to You! 181

11. Effective Meditation 185
A Meditation Catechism 185
Tame the Monkey 188
Changing Consciousness 188
Some Common Meditations 191
Gotama's Distinctive Mindfulness Meditation 192
Begin Where You Are 194
The Wind Beneath Our Wings 195
Over to You! 196

12. A Positive Psychology 199
Understanding How We Function 199
Describing the Five Clusters Process 201

An Encounter with Spiders..202
Facing Sudden Death..202
Skandha Analysis 203
Understanding Ourselves 205
A Buddhist Personality Test...206
The Main Motive..207
A New Stability 208
A Window on Our "Emptiness" 210
Over to You!..211

13. Character Development 215
Character Building 216
New Habits for a Renewed You..217
Replacing Unskilful Habits 218
Compassion Begins at Home 219
Free Agency and Dependency...220
Choose the Best Approach for You.....................................221
Strive for Six 'Perfections' 222
Pursuing a Multi-faceted Love 222
Over to You!..225

14. Living Like a Refugee 229
Our Need for a Refuge 229
The Original Refuge Seekers 231
A Triple Affirmation 233
Three-in-One 234
It's Not All About Gotama..234
Five Moral Precepts...235

A Fulsome Refuge 237
Seeking Refuge Makes Us Refugees 238
Over to You! 240

15. More Than Me and Mine 243
No-self (*anatta*) 244
Self-ish Barriers to Inner Freedom 245
The *Bodhisattva* Ideal 246
Archetypal Figures 248
Altruism Benefits the Giver 249
Evaluating Our Impact 250
Engaged with Social Needs 251
Ashoka's Example of Social Concern 253
Co-operation and Compromise 254
Many Charities Deserve Our Support 255
The Dark Side of Social Engagement 257
Over to You! 260

16. The Wheel of Life 263
An Educational and Motivational Mural 263
Four Circles, Two Energies 265
The Innermost Circle 267
The Second Circle 267
Six Realms 268
The Realm of the Gods 269
The Realm of the Titans 270
The Animal Realm 271
The Hell Realm 272

The Realm of the Hungry Ghosts 272
The Human Realm 273
One Thing Leads to Another 273
A Contemporary Wheel of Life 276
We're Here for Good 277
Over to You! 278

17. Spiritual, Religious, or Both? 281
"I'm Spiritual but Not Religious" 282
How We Do Community is Crucial 283
Inevitable Ambiguities 284
Toxic and Wholesome Behaviours 286
Advantages of Religion: An Example 288
Transcendence 290
Do Buddhists Pray and Worship? 291
Deep Agnosticism 293
Spiritual, Secular, and Religious 294
Over to You! 295

Postlude 299
What Now? 299
Finding Our Own Path 300
Be Prepared to Change 301
A Parable of Self-discovery 303
Go For It! 305

Appendix: The First Turning of the *Dharma* Wheel, Paraphrased 309
Introduction 309

The Discourse	310
The Gods Rejoice	314
About the Author	316
Rebalance Your Life for Contentment and Attainment	319
Notes and References	321

Letter to a Friend

Dear Alex,

You know me well enough to realise I couldn't be happier with your questions, "What is Buddhism?" and "What does it offer?" And I know you well enough to trust that you're seeking something more than simplistic answers or the superficial happiness that many promote these days. Perhaps you, like me, have been disillusioned by offers that promise more than they can deliver.

Around six centuries before Jesus, The Buddha (his given name was Siddartha Gotama) shared his insights on living the best possible life. Buddhism's vitality comes from his original wisdom and the many different insights of his disciples, from his time to ours. We can join his original teachings with those from a variety of other sources.

Some commonly held thoughts about Buddhism need challenging. For instance, meditation is often thought to be the be all and end all. Although he saw meditation as crucially important, it was just one part of a multidimensional understanding of how to gain a fruitful and peaceful life. The central, pervasive theme of his teaching was transformational change through a variety of practices to benefit ourselves and others.

What does Buddhism offer? The traditional term is "happiness" (*sukha* in the original language). Perhaps it's better translated as well-being, contentment, or flourishing. The opposite of *sukha* is *dukkha*, which means ill-being, stress, dissatisfaction, and suffering. You might say his teaching is about replacing *dukkha* with *sukha*. It takes us far beyond popular concepts of happiness and personal growth!

After six years of earnest searching, the Buddha found reliable patterns and potentials for positive living. He discovered a radically new understanding of the meaning of 'self'. He determined how we can escape what many term "existential anxiety". Not that a life lived apart from his insights is utterly miserable and ineffective! There are many positives in every way of life, philosophy or religion, and we need not abandon them.

His teaching is not a "revelation from heaven" but the experience of an exceptional human being. He thought deeply about his own life and what he observed in others, and from that drew some unprecedented conclusions. He was also immensely practical in describing how we can have a fruitful and fulfilling life, drawing upon everything that helps us help ourselves. Some of these teachings might seem obvious; others are quite mysterious until we start to test their effectiveness for ourselves.

It's quite an adventure, this life-long learning called Buddhism. He called it *bodhi* (Awakening).

Friends always!

Dennis

Preface

The Buddha's teachings lead us towards contentment, flourishing, fundamental well-being, and a profound, holistic happiness. His path to Awakening has proved relevant to more than a billion people, over 2.5 millennia – mostly in Asia, but increasingly in the West today.

In presenting what the Buddha said and did, I have drawn primarily on translations of the early scriptures of the Buddhist tradition.[3] These were written in the ancient Pali language (this is more colloquial than Sanskrit) from the third to second century BCE. Whilst it is impossible to extract his exact words and life story from documents written more than three centuries after his death, from them, we can sense the basic shape of his teaching and its dynamic power. As well, I have drawn from other sources, ancient and contemporary, when they seem relevant.

I have also included contemporary photographs in each chapter. These are intended to pause the thought process with a different kind of reflection. They are meant to allow your imagination to blossom. An open and reflective approach is useful for considering the Buddha's thoughts, which, in the end, need to be understood and applied by each individual. Everything I share in this book is meant to prompt you to think for yourself. Blind agreement is a passion killer for any spiritual teaching.

What you read in this book is grounded in the Buddhist Scriptures. Yet I admit to presenting them with a pragmatic interpretation. I am sure this perspective will nurture many.

I have provided the source reference within the endnote section of the passages that I have used or paraphrased, taking special care when quoting the Buddha's words, due to the many false quotes attributed to him. Most endnotes were included to allow readers to check out the quotes in their original context. A few offer additional information.

There are many introductions to the Buddha's teachings. Each has its distinctive point of view, often at variance with the others. This is inevitable, no matter how carefully we do our research. Some may imply that their interpretation of Buddhism is the only accurate and authentic representation of what the Buddha said and did. I would not go that far but I am convinced by the helpfulness of this presentation.

My interpretation is underpinned by my strong belief that the Buddha intended us to find "Contentment Here and Now". For many the Buddhist message seems to be 'Avoid unethical, harmful actions now and you'll be better off in your next life.' In contrast, I'll highlight opportunities to continue (or, for some, begin) the process of Awakening in this lifetime. Each positive step or stage in this process often results in blessings and benefits – moving us towards the deepest possible contentment.

In sharing the Buddha's experiences and my own, I describe the journey of Awakening based on a secular Buddhist interpretation. This recognises that most of the the Buddha's teaching was about the life we are living right now in this world and not in a heavenly realm. The resultant experiences, especially in advanced forms of meditation, may be described as 'celestial'. But the heavenly dimension of Awakening is a metaphor for the satisfaction and fulfilment that comes from following the Buddhist path wholeheartedly and without compromise. The feeling is real, but it is firmly grounded in our human experience.

I freely admit that my emphasis on the here and now seems to contradict a small portion of the teachings recorded in the early documents. It is important to recognise their nature (memories and assertions passed orally through many generations for 300-400 years before they became 'Scripture'. It is likely that some distortions and additions have occurred. Without the arrogance of certainty, I wonder if some of the more supernatural and celestial passages were 'remembered' in terms of popular other-worldly concepts.

These Scriptures are not thought to be infallible, inerrant revelations. Rather they are devout presentations of the Buddha's teaching. The commentaries on the originals seem to show that the monks were not shy to add their own content to the Buddha's words. I am very respectful of the text but have concluded that my interpretive framework is in keeping with the original intention. However, I recognise that no one can know with certainty what the Buddha said, word for word. What is important in the teaching is not so much its source as its ability to direct us towards healthy, helpful, happy living.

Within the community of Buddhist understandings and emphases lies a strong emphasis on our individual judgments about its efficacy and effectiveness[4]. As we shall see, the Buddha's advice is that we avoid mindless, slavish acceptance of his views or indeed the views of anyone else. Rather, we are invited to follow his guidance only when and if it rings true to our experience and reflects the wisdom of those we respect.

I view Buddhism through four lenses: **pragmatic, secular, spiritual,** and **cosmopolitan**.

Gotama, the Buddha, was **PRAGMATIC**. A pragmatic Buddhism does not look for an eternal, abstract and disembodied "truth" but for understandings which will help us improve ourselves and others. I concur with Shurendra Ghimire, a devout Buddhist scholar:

"Buddhism is closest to pragmatism among modern philosophies. Pragmatism is supposed as a suggestion for developing and redeveloping ideas for practical use rather than a philosophical stand of its own fixed realm."[5]

The Buddha's message was essentially **SECULAR**, although it avoids some common limitations associated with the word. By secular, I do not mean narrowly materialist, nor dismissive of spirituality. Secular is a word from the Latin *saeculum*, meaning "of the world; of this generation". Our focus is on the Buddha's teaching for the life we're living, not for a future paradise.

The Buddhist Path can be described as a pilgrimage towards **SPIRITUAL** realities. Spirituality takes us far beyond our five senses and our sense-based reasoning, to intuitions and emotions that are not fully encompassed by scientific measurement. In Buddhism these energies are not derived from a personal God (Creator/Saviour/Judge). However, some Buddhists refer to an immeasurable 'Universal Mind', 'Supra-personal Force', or even 'God' (but not in the ordinary use of the term). I personally sense a 'life force' (call it what you will) within the universe that touches my humanity deeply. Buddhism points to a positive energy beyond our own: an energy that is indescribable yet able to be experienced if we are open to it.

My approach is decidedly **COSMOPOLITAN**. Buddhism provides a framework to discover a multitude of insights about human flourishing from non-Buddhist sources. Concepts, such as emotional intelligence, the hierarchy of needs, and the findings of modern psychology and neurology, help us towards expanding our ability to flourish. These were unknown to the Buddha, but I'm sure he would have welcomed such new knowledge had he been aware of it. That said, this study is mainly focused on his teaching. It is not attempting to integrate the relevant data from the religions, arts, and sciences.

In this book I am sharing how and why I find Buddhism so meaningful and practical in my own life and the positive growth I have seen it make in other peoples' lives. Each one of us has a unique story. I count my discovery of Buddhist understandings as the most crucial source for my present well-being. My hope is that these examples will be a stimulant to finding an appropriate spirituality well suited to yourself.

The overall purpose of this book is to prompt you to walk the path of Awakening. It's quite the journey, and I commend it to you. As an encouragement to this kind of growth I have included an "Over to You" section at the end of each chapter, with questions to consider.

Dennis Oliver (Seng Ting)
Glasgow
Buddha Day 2025

Acknowledgements

If I tried to acknowledge every helpful input which has informed this book, it would inevitably omit many significant contributors. But neither should I fail to mention some people and communities that have been crucial in progressing this project.

Brian Duffy, my Editor, has provided me with innumerable penetrating and independent perceptions of the best way to express my insights. As well, Brian has provided some of the book's diagrams. This would have been a much weaker book without his reshaping. He is a perfectionist in the best sense of the word.

Ian Noble has been an active partner in this project. He has provided the book's contemporary photos and diagrams. He has contributed many insights that have helped to shape and amplify my thoughts as well as an unfailing encouragement to write.

Vairocana, an Order member of the Triratna Buddhist Community, has been a keen student of the *dharma* from age seventeen. His input has always been helpful and encouraging. Not only did he answer my specific questions, but he often drew my attention to relevant *suttas* that were new to me.

Elizabeth, my wife, has supported my writing preoccupation but also helped me to get away from it when I needed to. Though not a Buddhist, she has been a model for many of the qualities that contribute to a spiritually informed human flourishing.

The Amida, Triratna, and the Pragmatic Buddhism *sanghas* have provided spiritual 'base camps' from which I have ventured out on my own. The members of the Centre for Pragmatic Buddhism in Scotland have been crucial to the maturing of this book, helping me to refine my ideas, providing new insights into applying and explaining how Buddhist teaching can enrich our real-time living.

The prisoners of HMP Kilmarnock played an essential part in shaping my pragmatism. The idea for writing this book began during a series of talks at the prison aimed at introducing a practical Buddhism for non-monastics. The prisoners' responsiveness (often, but not always, affirming) encouraged me to keep going with this project. I am grateful for their influence.

Some of my understandings have been trialled with the Spiritual Naturalist Society[6], the Secular Buddhist Network[7], and the Middle Way Society.[8]

The writings and seminars of Sangharakshita, Stephen Batchelor and Thich Nhat Hanh have also contributed much to my understanding.

Most of all, I am thankful for the teaching and example of the one who discovered what we now call Buddhism, lived it, and shared it - the Buddha. I hope this little book allows his examples and insights to register as an effective aid to your growth and flourishing.

All this is not to avoid taking responsibility for every word in the book. I welcome any factual corrections, notice of copywriting violations, misattributions, or typos. Please send your comments to dennis.oliver.me@gmail.com

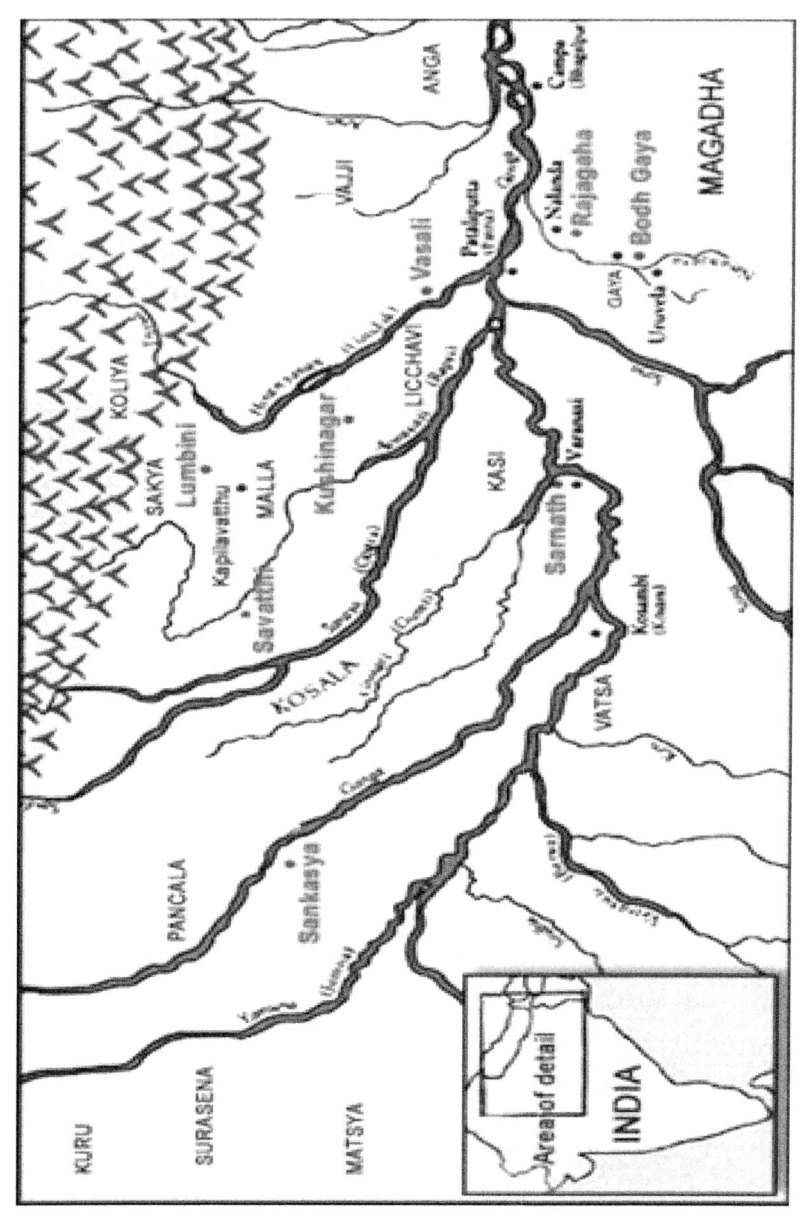

Map of the Buddha's India, 500 BCE[9]

A Secular Buddhist Spirituality

Reflection: Beginner's Mind

The 'Mona Lisa Buddha'[10]

Prelude

"This Stuff Really Works!"

Buddhism has changed and sustained me since 2006. This is when I began to take its practical wisdom seriously. My confidence in the relevance of the Buddha's teachings kept growing as I applied them. And this was further reinforced as I saw how others changed for the better through the same *dharma*.

Dharma is an ancient Indian word that encapsulates two key elements: the Buddhist teaching and its lived experience. If we just understand concepts such as compassion or equanimity without experiencing them, we've not really got the point the Buddha was making. But when we "get it" we realise how powerfully positive life can be. When we discover the experience behind its concepts and claims, the *dharma* is almost always better than we expect.

In my nine-year prison chaplaincy at HMP Kilmarnock, two examples of *dharma* learning stand out. Scott and Billy (not their real names) were in my class on Buddhist Meditation. They never took on the "Buddhist" label. But each, in their own way, absorbed and applied something 100 times more important.

Billy was a keen student in my prison meditation class. He left it when he was released, but a few months later, he was sent back to prison. An old offence had caught up with him. I chanced upon him on my visits, and he collared me. "You need to hear my story!" he insisted. I certainly did! Soon after leaving prison, Billy became deeply hooked on heroin, returning to his past habit. But he was hungry for a better life. He decided to kick his addiction cold turkey, stopping abruptly and unassisted. No one would have advised that!

Billy told me that he drew on the various meditation practices he'd learned in class. He stayed as mindful as he could, finding the strength to endure the agonies of withdrawal. Once he was through that hellish process, Billy showed himself to be one of the finest men I've known. His articulation of Buddhist principles was different from mine. But he could apply them with near-miraculous effectiveness. As well as escaping his heroin habit, Billy stayed positive and productive in a most challenging environment. He became an unofficial pastor to his peers, respected for his wisdom and kindness.

Another of my students, Scott, was put in prison following some trouble he got himself into after returning "broken" (his word) from military service in Afghanistan, where he had served as a sniper. His wounds were not external. Flashbacks haunted him – reliving his killings as much as the brutality experienced by his comrades. At the beginning of the class, Scott shared that he needed relief from 'anxiety' – a word that hardly did justice to his post-traumatic stress disorder.

After ten appearances, he stopped coming, and I thought I hadn't been able to help him. But the opposite was true. He had been attending a class required for his release. When Scott completed it, he returned to our mindfulness lessons with enthusiasm for its power to transform lives. It provided reliable relief from his anxiety. His message to the others was, "This stuff really works! It changed my life. It will change yours – if you let it."

I have also seen how aspects of the approach presented in the following chapters work in a variety of circles, including recovery groups, religious communities, and secular organisations, as well as in the lives of many unaffiliated individuals.

Retain Your Individuality

The original Buddha of 5th Century India, Siddartha Gotama, discovered an approach to living that brought him everything he had been seeking. Once gained and savoured, he shared his experiences with others, communicating broad principles which allow and encourage individual interpretations and applications.

Gotama was as human as you or me, but he learned to transcend the ordinary limits of his humanity. The records of his life show that after his transformation (Awakening), he retained many elements of his personality, which were influenced by his family, his culture, and his experiences. Those touched by his radical message also retained their individuality.

As traditions develop, they often try to impose strict rules and regulations about how we should think and act. Whilst Gotama taught what thoughts and actions were helpful and what were harmful, he left the application and its consequences to each of us. For example, he taught that "sexual misconduct" is to be avoided and "meditation" practised. But what that means in practice has been answered quite differently by different Buddhist traditions, with even more variety from their members!

Rigid, legalistic demands are dull prose compared to the poetry of individual responses. In my experience with all types of organisations – religious, ideological, and political – some press their members to conform to inflexible systems without recognising their needs and potential. But others offer well-established insights yet allow participants to renew and expand their lives in ways that suit their individuality. The original Buddhist message encourages us to make individual applications. Each of us can find and follow, even create, a unique way forward into the full potential of our humanity informed by his teaching.

Make His Teachings Your Own

The original Buddhist teaching was not a set of propositions to affirm or believe. It is more like a spiritual self-development guide, with examples from real-life situations. Those who have applied it commonly comment that the teaching was familiar – it resonated with their sense of reality. When tried, it increases our vitality and sense of fulfilment, often in unexpected ways.

Once we begin this journey, the *dharma* steers us. Its instructions are so much more than a series of concepts or commands. Rather we have suggestions to explore, which leave us free to interpret and even modify them to suit our situation. Yet there is a recognisable pattern to the teaching. It demands wholehearted application and responds by opening a gateway to a fulfilling and fruitful life.

My Buddhist journey has been one of both gradual and sudden changes in which I have learned to see myself and others in a more positive and hopeful light. I am confident that you can embrace the same dynamic.

Do What is Helpful for You

The essential purpose of the *dharma* is to connect us to its transformative concepts. Then we can apply them in a way that works best for us.

The Buddha's insistence on our deciding our response to his teaching is underscored by a discourse describing a visit of some youthful enquirers, who were intrigued by the Buddha's reputation. When he entered their town, a group of Kalamas (their clan name) respectfully asked, how could they tell what philosopher or spiritual teacher was right and who was wrong, as each claimed that they alone had the correct view!

In response, the Buddha did not discuss the many different understandings that were competing for the attention of the Kalamas. Nor did he try to persuade them that his teaching was 'the best'. Rather, he told them to decide on the basis of what proved true and effective in their lives:

"Come, Kalamas. Do not be influenced by what you've taken on through repeated hearing; nor by tradition; nor by rumour; nor what is in a scripture; nor upon speculation; nor upon mere logic; nor prejudgement; nor untested ideas; nor the authority of your teacher.

"Kalamas, when you yourselves know, 'These things are good; these things are not blameable; these things are praised by the wise; their benefits have been observed in real lives; they lead to happiness' then it only makes sense to practise them and keep on doing so."[11]

In effect he was saying, 'Make your minds up on the basis of what is helpful to you and to those you know and respect.'

Buddhists are not meant to be blindly following what they have not seen to work in their own and others' lives.

A Positive Basis for Change

Sometime after the Buddha's death, the idea of Buddha Nature was articulated. It has been interpreted in many ways, providing an empowering and energising self-concept for many. According to this concept, we all can become as Awake as the Buddha! It's a potential for anyone willing to be as serious and disciplined.

The evolution of human consciousness has a spiritual dimension. Many today have moved from a tribal and national self-concept towards identifying with the wider human family. Others move from a focus on relational, material and financial security towards a quest for meaning, mystical experience, and a deeper, consciousness of themselves and the world. Just as humanity has evolved from wandering tribes to settlements, then cities, our consciousness is evolving too.

The concepts of Buddha Nature and spiritual evolution[12] have helped me understand the significance of the Buddha's teaching.

Open to Other Helpful Models

Our cosmopolitan approach to spirituality can include non-Buddhist understandings. One is the idea of flourishing, as articulated within Dr. Martin Seligman's concept of Positive Psychology. It is supported by much research.[13]

Seligman coined the acronym 'PERMA' to describe what he means by flourishing:

P represents **Positive emotions** such as satisfaction, awe, joy, and contentment.

E is for **Engagement**; this relates to our experience of flow (being absorbed by an activity).

R, for **Relationships**, refers to the quality and quantity of social connections inside and outside our immediate group.

M refers to **Meaning**: having a sense of purpose or meaning in life.

A, points to **Accomplishment** which is based on the experience of achievement and progression toward goals.[14]

A second model that informs this study is Dr. Jeffery Martin's research about people he calls 'Finders'[15]: women and men who experience an abiding "fundamental well-being". Some were Buddhists, others Christian, agnostics, atheist, and adherents of a wide variety of spiritual, religious, and philosophical understandings. Common terms the Finders used to describe their well-being were enlightenment (seeing the pervasive truth of the universe), nonduality (persistent unitive consciousness) and mystical experience (inner peace at a profound level, "the peace that passes understanding"[16] which is present in the higher consciousness that many experience in meditation).

Our cosmopolitan approach articulates and supplements much of what Gotama taught. There are so many alternative views from a wide variety of sources which can inform our journey towards Awakening. It's only reasonable to be open to their helpful insights. For example, I find the Christian emphasis on identifying with the vulnerable and oppressed in society helpful in its challenge to avoid promoting the social status quo and favouring the rich and powerful.

Yet I and many others find the Buddha's analysis and practices, realistic and accessible. All his teaching is rooted in human experience. I can test, adapt, and embrace them enthusiastically. I am eternally grateful for the frame of reference he provided in his core teachings, as reflected in this book. But I am also encouraged to know that the Buddha was describing what others, from different times and cultures, were also discovering. That the *dharma* bears some resemblance to the subsequent teachings of many Sages and Adepts reinforces its longevity, utility and value.

A Certain Smile

The journey to Awakening is not meant to be grim and exhausting. Every step, whether hearing the practical teaching or applying it, brings its own sense of pleasure. There are challenges as we reorient our thoughts and actions and see ourselves in a more realistic context, but the overall experience discovers and expresses the best in us. It is a process marked by joy – sometimes quiet and subtle, sometimes exuberant. The depictions of the historical Buddha and his disciples often depict a smile, reflecting the inward-outward contentment they are experiencing.

The 'Mona Lisa Buddha' (shown at the beginning of this chapter) is one of the best-known examples. This Asian "archaic smile" is meant to convey ease and well-being, something beyond the bright, even giddy smiles in modern media advertising. The 'happiness' of Buddhists often begins with deeply felt expressions of rapture, including goosebumps. But as we learn to meditate at deeper levels, the smile becomes quieter and subtler. This yields a profound contentment in our bodies, emotions, and thoughts.

We might say that the purpose of this book is to show how to put a smile of contentment on your face, if it's not already there.

Over to You!

You will have had your own deeply felt experiences. They will have informed and energised every aspect of your life. Their source is found in your human nature, which includes an immense potential for a truly contented life. You might start a journal to collect your thoughts about the principles and practices that have proved effective for over 2500 years.

1. In what ways does your unique personal story shape what you are seeking from yourself and others?

2. How would you like Buddhism to contribute to both your needs and your aspirations?

CONTENTMENT HERE AND NOW

3.

Refection: What Now?

The Birth of the Buddha[17]

1.
Everything Was Not Enough

"The traditional story of the Buddha's life may not be factually accurate; we have no way to know for certain. Historians today generally agree there was a historical Buddha and that he lived in the 4th through 6th centuries BCE, give or take. It's believed that at least some of the sermons and monastic rules recorded in the oldest scriptures are his words or something close to his words. But that's as far as most historical scholars will go."
Barbara O'Brien[18]

The Man Behind the Myth

Behind the Buddhist scriptures and traditions stands an extraordinary human being. For more than two and a half millennia after his death, his practical insights have transformed individuals and cultures. From the available evidence, we conclude that he was a charismatic teacher who proclaimed liberation and demanded radical change. He taught a range of qualities, including goodwill, compassion, freedom, contentment, generosity, courage – and the means of gaining them. But he also conveyed a new way of experiencing life and understanding the nature of ourselves and the wider universe. He was a spiritual revolutionary.

Gotama, the man who became Buddha, is recognised as one of the world's great philosophers and the founder of a movement and way of life that once commanded the loyalty of up to one-third of humanity. Today, over half a billion people call themselves Buddhists. Collectively they form the fourth largest 'religion' on earth. His teaching inspires many, many more.

Some people are shocked to hear that the thousands of Buddhist Scriptures were compiled and codified after ten or more generations of monks passed on Gotama's experiences and discourses by word of mouth, from memory. These recollections of his life and his discourses have been supplemented by legends and interpretations which were clearly not his own. This 'history' was inevitably framed from a faith perspective and coloured by the tradition of the monk's community.

Buddhists do not believe their Scriptures are "revelations" with God-guaranteed veracity.

When we share his traditional story, you'll notice that ancient Indian storytellers were often less focused on historical accuracy and more intent on conveying their deep convictions about the Buddha's significance.

What really matters is the utility of the teachings. For millennia Buddhists have celebrated their liberating effect, and their power to transform us. They certainly have served me and many of my Buddhist friends well.

Taken as a whole, the Buddhist Scriptures and added traditions picture an extraordinary man who dedicated his life to discovering and then sharing his unprecedented understanding of liberation and flourishing. But in some parts, the texts seem to make of him something that he never claimed to be, namely a miracle-working god-like being who became the object of worship and supplication for hundreds of millions of his Asian followers. Even the earliest documents (written in Pali, a language close to what he would have spoken) occasionally present him as a miracle-maker. Did he teleport, levitate, visit gods and his mother in heavenly realms, and create a jewelled staircase in the sky?[19]

I, for one, am inspired and informed by a different kind of Buddha whose life and teaching showed how ordinary humans can be transformed. The truth is, we'll never know what hard facts are contained within these pious portrayals. But it is possible to extract from them a coherent set of teachings (the *dharma*).

When I speak of Gotama, the Buddha, I focus on his core teachings more than his life story. But we can still embrace those stories that touch us deeply, even the ones which seem clearly unhistorical. Much within the early scriptures connects with our longing for a sense of one so 'special' – whose teachings are more credible and nurturing than any teacher we've encountered before.

A Miracle Child!

The traditional story is that Gotama was born within sight of the Himalayas in Kapilavastu, the capital of the Sakya Republic, which lived under the protection of the emerging empire of Kosala, West of Kapilavastu. He was the son of the *Raj* (King) Suddhodana and Queen Maya who is said to have become pregnant after dreaming a white elephant entered her side (this is one of many elaborated parts to the historical recollections). Nine months later, he emerged from the same place. In a few days, the baby began to walk.

With each step, a lotus flower appeared. He then declared, "I am chief of the world, eldest in the world, foremost in the world. This birth is my last." He announced the same as he strode in each of the four directions (North, South, East, West) to declare his prominence and pre-eminence among all of humanity.

Maya died a week after her son's birth. Her sister, Mahapajapati, raised the little prince. This loss must have profoundly affected the boy. A story arose that he visited his mother, after she was reborn in one of the realms of the 'gods' (*devas*).

Soon after the boy was born, *Raj* Suddhodana called in astrologers and seers to determine his destiny. One of them, a family priest, Asita, began to weep for joy: "Sire, your son will grow to be either a world-honoured spiritual leader or a world-conquering monarch!" The others concurred. The child was given the name Siddhattha (Siddhartha in Sanskrit), meaning "he who has found his purpose". Gotama was his clan name.

Asita's Prediction[20]

Raj Suddhodana, Gotama's father, was pleased with the significance attributed to his son but also worried: What if the boy rejected the royal role and became a religious zealot? He and his kingdom needed a strong son and heir to rule after him, undistracted by any other sense of mission. To this end, he trained Gotama in both statecraft and the arts of war. The story takes on a fairy-tale flavour: The boy became the best bowman in the land, winning the hand of his bride Yasodhara in an archery contest.

A Pampered Youth

To prevent his only son and heir from renouncing his responsibilities as a future ruler, *Raj* Suddhodana gave him the best his world could offer: wealth, power, prestige, and pleasure. These were the perks the *Raj* enjoyed. He did everything possible to keep the prince from life's difficulties and sorrows.

Gotama received the best education available, resulting in a mind as informed and acute as any ancient philosopher. Taxila, a city southwest of Kapilavastu, hosted the area's leading 'university'. Likely, the young prince was trained there. He enjoyed the privileges of being the *Raj's* son and was indulged in every possible way. Looking back on this time, after his Awakening, Gotama reflected,

> "I lived in total refinement. My father's palace included three lotus ponds: one where red lotus bloomed, the others for white and blue lotus – all for my sake. I used no sandalwood except the highest quality. My turban was from Varanasi, the best and most expensive, as were my tunic, pants, and outer cloak. Servants attended me day &

night to remove the effects of cold and heat, dust and dew."[21]

Right from his early years, the young Gotama was sensitive and caring for other beings. His compassionate character is described in a story about a conflict with his cousin Devadatta, as they played with their bows and arrows. When a goose flew near, Devadatta shot it and then ran over to finish the kill. But the young prince intervened, saying the goose could be brought back to health. "It's my right to finish what I've begun", insisted his cousin. "But the goose can be saved," insisted young Gotama. They argued back and forth until Gotama suggested they go to his father to decide and tenderly carried the bird to the palace. *Raj* Suddhodana sided with his son, and the bird was placed in the care of the royal household. Kindness and compassion had prevailed.

The times in which he lived were brutal, with many conflicts arising. Perhaps the young Gotama was too sensitive to relish the dynamics of autocratic warrior-like leadership expected of a young prince in ancient India.

The Legend of the Four Sights

Tired of the overprotection of his father, the young prince ordered his charioteer, Channa, to take him outside the palace walls to get a fuller view of his people. For the first time in his life, he was confronted with the stark realities of life when he saw four people. This is known as the Four Sights.

A Secular Buddhist Spirituality

Three of the Four Sights. Contemporary painting[22]

The first sight was an elderly person bent over a stick to ease walking pain. "What is that, Channa?" "An old man, sire." "That is so pitiful, Channa, and how does it happen?" "We just wait for it, sire. We will grow old and feeble unless we die young." "Will this happen to you, Channa?" "It comes to all of us, sire." "Even me?" "Even you!" Prince Gotama was shaken by the news that the pleasures he enjoyed would end. The same realisation came to him when he saw a sick person (second sighting) and a funeral procession (the third). All that sustained him in life was no protection from its inescapable raw realities: old age, sickness, and death.

Then Gotama saw a fourth person, a man in saffron robes with a begging bowl. He seemed quite different from what he had been observing. There was a calmness and a sense of deep satisfaction in the man. "Who is he, Channa? He seems so unusual." Channa answered "He is a holy man. He is seeking a deeper understanding of what our lives are all about. Some people leave everything for this search." This man was a robed wanderer dedicated to finding liberation (*moksha*), for which he had abandoned the ordinary expectations and obligations to society and his family.

At that time, many were joining the growing number of wandering seekers, called *shramanas* (those 'who exert effort and austerities for a higher purpose').[23] They were also known as *bhikkhus* ("beggars") because they relied on others for their food. They sought something they felt was lacking from the Brahman priests or Vedic doctrines and exclusive ritualistic practices. Gotama seemed impressed by their example.

The prince who had everything the world could offer, anguished over what he lacked. He yearned for a sense of existential security, inner peace, and conviction that he was on the right path. The Four Sights legend represents a real existential crisis that the prince experienced around the time he became a new father. Perhaps he felt he could provide the child, as a suitable heir for his father. He had named his son Rahula, which has been translated as "a fetter [restraint] to enlightenment".[24] He was resisting a settled and prescribed life. Seeing him questioning the meaning of life and death over a more extended period than the legend implies, humanises the story.

Going Forth (The Great Renunciation)

Relief Showing Prince Siddhartha's Great Departure[25]

In an autobiographical statement, Gotama confided,

> "Before my Awakening... being myself subject to birth, sought what was likewise subject to birth. Myself subject to ageing, illness, death, sorrow, and defilement, I sought [happiness in] what was likewise subject to them. The thought occurred to me, 'Why do I seek such things? What if I sought the ageing-less, illness-less, death-less, sorrow-less?'

> "So, at a later time, while still young, a black-haired young man endowed with the blessings of youth in the first stage of life — and while my parents, unwilling, were crying with tears streaming down their faces — I shaved off my hair & beard, put on the ochre robe and went forth from the home life into homelessness."[26]

Despite his situation's many benefits and responsibilities, Gotama left the palace and became a wandering seeker. He rode to the border of his Kingdom, cut off his beautiful hair and exchanged clothes with an impoverished woodsman. Some use the term 'renunciation' because he renounced his pleasures, securities, and privileges to find something more satisfying. Gotama began his search, walking through the northern Indian subcontinent.

What was the object of this bold move away from all the securities he had enjoyed? It was, he said, a search for "ageing-less, illness-less, death-less, sorrow-less". Was he really looking for the secret to perfect health, everlasting youth, freedom from anguish, and eternal life? Or was his object the Eternal One who enjoyed all these qualities? In our time we might call the latter 'God'. In his context, the search might have been for Brahma, understood as a universal force within us and the universe, yearning to be united. We really don't know. But this was simply the beginning of a long search. His understanding likely would have changed over the six years of his pre-awakened searching.

One early incident involved an interview with a young *Raj*, King Bimbisara of Rajagriha Bimbisara, who recognised the remarkable nature of Gotama and asked him to be his Prime Minister. Gotama explained his quest and promised to return if he found the secret of true happiness. True to his word, the newly awakened Buddha later returned to report his discovery, and he and the Raj developed a lifelong friendship. But Gotama still had no desire to return to a worldly role.

Six Long Years of Searching

For six years, he rubbed shoulders with fellow seekers, discussing and debating the meaning of life. Early on, he was attracted to two leading meditation teachers, well thought of at the time for their mastery of altered states of consciousness through meditation. Alara Kalama taught Gotama how to reach "the sphere of no-thingness". Uddaka Ramaputta showed him how to reach an even higher (deeper) level termed "the sphere of neither perception nor non-perception". Gotama mastered these techniques so well that each teacher invited him to teach their disciples. But he saw that these meditations had brought no lasting transformation. He had not left his relatives and inheritance just to enjoy temporary delights! He was seeking a more comprehensive improvement.

He left his teachers and continued searching, but he could find no credible replacements to Alara Kalama and Uddaka Ramaputta; no one taught meditation better than they. So, he embraced a common option taken up by some of the most serious and rigorous *shramanas*: extreme asceticism, denying his basic need for food. A legend claimed that eventually, he took only one grain of rice a day! A well-known sculpture depicts his weakened body.

Gotama after years of austerity[27]

Sujata's Life-Giving Gift

Gotama finally came to his senses. He realised that these austerities were fruitless. Thus, he escaped the inevitable consequences of such extreme actions (death). The legend of Sujata is a beautiful depiction of this momentous redirection.

Sujata offers Rice Balls to Gotama[28]

A heartwarming story (not in the oldest documents) is that the emaciated Gotama fell into a river while washing himself. He was so weak he could not rise and likely would have died. But a servant girl, Sujata, passed by. Her name translates as "milkmaid". She was carrying milk and rice to offer at the nearby family shrine. Her heart went out to Gotama, and she dragged him to safety, then fed him with her ritual offering. Her common sense and compassion made Gotama realise how wrong he had been to deny himself the food he needed to maintain his strength – and that denying his basic needs was not helpful. He abandoned this dangerous extremism to gain more energy for his search. Sujata kept feeding him until he was well enough to move on.

Gotama altered his diet thereafter to include at least one full meal a day. This strengthened both his body and his mind. He then was more able to devote himself to his search for "the deathless".

Over to You!

1. How do you understand the more poetic (mythic and legendary) aspects of this story?

2. Are there parts of Gotama's story that speak to you deeply?

Reflection: A Shadowy Shelter

Gotama's Breakthrough[29]

2.
Forty-five Years of Being Buddha

"The Blessed One is worthy and rightly self-awakened, consummate in knowledge and conduct, well-gone, an expert about the world, unexcelled as a trainer for those people fit to be tamed."
Mahanama Sutta[30]

"What humanity owes to personalities like Buddha, Moses, and Jesus ranks for me higher than all the achievements of the enquiring and constructive mind. What these blessed men have given us we must guard and try to keep alive with all our strength if humanity is not to lose its dignity, the security of its existence, and its joy in living."
Albert Einstein[31]

His Great Awakening

Gotama found a pleasant place for a do-or-die effort to reach his goal of discovering the deathless (the eternal) through concentrated reflection. Later he came to call the goal of the spiritual life, *nirvana* - a "blowing out" of all that leads to suffering - a synonym for full Awakening. If he began his search with a desire to discover contentment through some external power, it ended when he found all that he needed within himself.

He was weary of false and partial understandings. His six years as a wandering seeker had certainly simplified his life. But all the debates, discussions, and solitary musings – even the dramatic shifts of consciousness from his meditations and ascetic practices – did not bring the insight and comfort he sought. Perhaps an answer would emerge from a meditation which went beyond all these unfulfilling practices.

Seated beneath a huge tree, on a mat he made from the gift of a grass cutter, Gotama reflected on the different theories and practices presented to him by fellow wanderers he had met over the past six years. While meditating, he faced his greatest fears and temptations. Mara, the Buddhist devil figure (representing the unconscious, conflicting forces within us) tried to undermine him by asking, "What right do you have to seek such a goal?" Gotama imagined the earth goddess rising and confirming his heroic efforts. Then, Mara sent his armies to attack him. Gotama's serenity was such that the arrows and spears turned to flowers. Mara's last attempt was to present his four daughters, each with their special sensual enticement, in Gotama's mind. But Gotama would not abandon his quest. After overcoming Mara, his mind began to sort out the way forward.

A key realisation came as he considered human nature, including the instinctual reactions to experience. Why do people behave the way we do? Gotama expressed this in terms of the assumption that each of us has emerged from countless past lives. Gotama reviewed his past in great detail, distinguishing what was wise from what was foolish.

He saw when and how his behaviours and thoughts were skilful and when they were not. Then, he reviewed the life patterns of others in the same way.

Gotama realised that people are driven by emotions and reactions which are often out of touch with reality ("the way things really are"). Some are unprofitably hostile, such as when we react with uncontrolled anger, hatred, or jealousy. Some are dangerously attractive, often resulting in obsessive and excessive desires. All come from an ignorance of what lies behind human dynamics. (We explore this in our chapter on Buddhist Psychology.)

"I am Awake"

Gradually, the fog cleared. Gotama began to see the realities leading to liberation. He considered the nature of human existence, how we resist our available freedom, and how we misinterpret our place in the universe.

When Dona, a Brahmin, met the new Buddha, he marvelled at his shining presence. On seeing him, he went to him and inquired who he really was,

> "Master, are you a *deva* [a divine being]?"
> "No, brahmin, I am not a *deva*."
> "Are you a *gandhabba* [a celestial being]?"
> "No..."
> "... a *yakkha* [a nature spirit]?"
> "No..."
> "... a human being?"
> "No, brahmin, I am not [an ordinary] human being."
> "Then what sort of being are you?"
> "I am Awake."[32]

Making Sense of It All

At first, Gotama could not believe anyone would grasp his insights.

> "This insight is deep. It's hard to see and harder to realise - simply too subtle for most. Yet it is so wonderful: peaceful, refined, self-evident. The wise can experience it. But this generation delights in their attachments, finding them exciting and delightful. For them, conditionality and dependent co-arising are hard to see… If I were to teach what I've learned and find that no one understands me, that would be tiresome and troublesome."[33]

This hesitation prompted an eruption from Gotama's subconscious (or perhaps his 'superconscious'), which saw that some people were ready to hear and accept his insights. He put it to his followers in a mythic story: Brahma Sahampati (a high god in the ancient Indian pantheon) appeared and pleaded with him not to keep his liberating message to himself. "Lord, let the Blessed One teach the *dharma*! Let the One-Well-Gone teach the *dhamma*! There are beings with little dust in their eyes falling away because they do not hear. Some will understand."[34]

This realisation shifted Gotama's focus to the positive. Just as a lotus pond has plants that have risen from the mud into the light – with others still immersed in the water, some would be ready to understand and keen to learn.

How can we explain Gotama's Awakening? His *dharma* points us to wisdom, a reality that speech and symbols can indicate, but not communicate fully. This "wisdom beyond words"[35] points us to perceptions and experiences which are inexpressible. Although his teaching nudges us towards Awakening, it remains a discovery that each must make individually. His *dharma* is "a finger pointing to the moon".[36] The moon indicates Awakening.

The First Disciples Were Laity

Soon after this transformative experience, Gotama encountered two commercial travellers, Tapussa and Bhallika. When he spoke of what had happened to him, it reoriented their lives.

Tapussa and Bhallika, became his first disciples. But they remained unordained, living with their families, as did multitudes of his followers. What we call laity were known as "householders" (*gihin*): men and women from all castes who were not monks. The monastic accounts evidence some stories of awakened laity but often give the impression that monastic life was the only path to enlightenment. But Awakening could be gained by anyone in any situation!

The learning community which Gotama nurtured consisted of four assemblies. The first two were monks and nuns, and the second pair were male and female householders. They and their descendants spread the liberating message far and wide over twenty-five centuries.

The early documents provide no statistics - but there were many thousands of monks and likely more lay followers by the end of Gotama's life. The *Gihi Sutta* (The Householder) speaks of a wealthy merchant, Anathapindika, "surrounded by about 500 lay followers" when he visited the Buddha.

The Growing Movement

When Gotama addressed his former ascetic colleagues, he explained how they, too, might Awaken. He outlined a multi-dimensional path that led to liberation and the mindset that puts us on it. His instruction was grounded in observations and reflections on his own experiences and others', rather than on 'pure reason'. It was full of general principles concerning the realities of human existence, allowing each person to apply their own insights to the broad directions that he gives. Thus it was relevant to the ordained and unordained.

In his day, the monks were wandering *bhikkhus* ("beggars") who were fed and otherwise sustained by alms from the villages and city dwellers. In exchange, they taught what they knew of the *dharma* and showed how Gotama's principles were a powerful model for well-being.

Lay merchants and missionary monks were both crucial for extending the liberating message. They shared the good news of Awakening. The Buddhist message was adapted and formulated to make sense within its new settings as it spread. In this way, hundreds of millions of people living beyond the Indian sub-continent understood the timeless message of Awakening.

A Master Teacher

Gotama was an exceptionally effective teacher. He travelled by foot through North India for forty-five years, rubbing shoulders with a wide variety of people, and developing an ability to communicate with labourers, merchants, and royalty. He could teach like Socrates (with an open-ended dialogue) or like a Rabbi (in declarative mode). He was not an academic in that he did not stress the sources of his concepts (which included some borrowed and modified Vedic teachings and much that was unique to him). Primarily, Gotama was 'pragmatic': stressing applications for living "this life" – not a future one.

Gold coin from Tillia Tepe, Ca. 100 BCE[37]
Inscription: *"The one who turned the Wheel of the Law"*

Gotama realised that we comprehend a new thought when it connects with something we already know. He spoke in parables, similes, and metaphors – all connected to what his audience could recognise. Suffering was "a bad wheel". The transformation we all need is an "Awakening". The self is like a "fire", which exists in a process that changes moment by moment. In the year he died, Gotama confided to a friend that he felt like "an old chariot, held together by ropes and rags".

One principle was to address people at the level of their understanding. He called it a "gradual" or "graduated" approach. If someone was not ready for wise perspectives or the disciplines of meditation, he might limit his message to moral conduct. To celibate monks, he mentioned the dangers and disadvantages of dwelling on sensual pleasures. But he never discouraged householders from appropriate (unharmful) sex.

The Buddha is well known for his down-to-earth illustrations. An example is his explanation of Awakening: 'It's like the experience of an explorer who discovers a path in the jungle. When he follows it to its end conclusion, he finds all the elements of a rich civilisation. What had been unproven rumours became a concrete reality, seen by direct knowledge.'[38]

Gotama's followers, lay and ordained, were surrounded by members of different sects. They all claimed confidently that they were right and all others wrong. His followers were upset and confused. In response, Gotama told the story of the Blind Men and the Elephant.

One felt the tusk and concluded that "An elephant is like a plough".

"No" said another who was feeling the tail's tuft. "It's rather like a broom."

A third who was feeling the elephant's massive flank insisted, "How wrong you are! An elephant is like a storeroom."[39]

A Secular Buddhist Spirituality

Blind men examining an elephant[40]

When Bahiya, an elderly wanderer who spent years seeking spiritual freedom, approached Gotama and asked for some teaching, he received this instruction:

> "If you see something, it's simply what you see. When you hear something, don't add to what you hear. Take the same approach for all the senses, including your thoughts. Don't daydream or speculate or add anything to the experience. That is the end of suffering." [41]

Through this brief *dharma* teaching of the Master, he freed the mind of Bahiya. It might be hard to imagine this having a life-changing significance, but it was just the right message for Bahiya.

His Last Months on Earth

The Aged Buddha[42]

Gotama faced much adversity in his final years. He endured a painful backache. Many of his friends and close associates died. He buried his own son. His cousin Devadatta plotted to lead his movement and tried twice to kill him. He nearly died of food poisoning. A long-standing disciple abandoned him. A neighbouring king destroyed his home city and slaughtered many of its residents. But Gotama calmly accepted it all. He had learned forty-five years before how to remove the unnecessary anguish, self-pity and hostility that so often accompanies such experiences.

Despite all these unfavourable circumstances, the whitehaired Gotama kept his focus on the continuation of his community and his message:

"Ananda, I've grown old; my journey is nearly over. I am almost eighty and feel it. Just as a worn-out cart is kept moving only with a lot of extra care, so my body can only keep going with a huge amount of will-power. "Therefore, Ananda, you all must be like islands. Be your own refuge – don't rely on another for your refuge. Make the *dhamma* your island and your refuge. Rely on no other. Whosoever seeks no external refuge, they of all my disciples shall reach the very topmost height! But they must be keen to progress."[43]

Though in significant discomfort, Gotama insisted they visit the monks to urge them to stick to the fundamental teachings:

"Such and such is virtue; such and such is concentration; and such and such is wisdom. A great gain comes from concentration when it is fully developed by virtuous conduct; the same can be said for wisdom when it is fully developed by concentration. The mind that is fully developed in wisdom is utterly freed from the taints of lust, becoming."[44]

In the same discourse, he chides his close companion Ananda for resisting the fact of his approaching death:

"Ananda, have I not taught from the very beginning that with all that is dear and beloved there must be change, separation, and severance? Of that which is born, come into being, is compounded and subject to decay, how can one say: 'May it not come to dissolution!' There can be no such state of things."[45]

Gotama was ready to go because he had prepared his followers to teach his *dharma*. He had determined to wait…

> "…until my monks and my lay followers, male and female, have become true disciples. They should be wise, well-disciplined, able and informed, preserving the *dharma*, living according to its guidance, with appropriate conduct. They need to be familiar with my teachings and able to teach it, preach it, proclaim it, and explain it in detail. It's meaning must be clear, so when opposing opinions arise, they can clarify meaning; when adverse opinions arise, they can refute them thoroughly and well, according to the liberating *dharma*."[46]

Since this *dharma* vision had been fulfilled in the lives of full-timers and laity (male and female), his vision had been fulfilled, so he was ready to die:

> "Before long my *parinibbana* [leaving his earthly existence] will have happened. Three months hence I shall utterly pass away."[47]

Despite his pains and feebleness, Gotama visited many of his disciples for the last time. On this 'tour', he suffered from persistent dysentery but recovered. Finally, he settled in a small village, Kushinagar. On his deathbed, he encouraged his gathered followers to ask him any questions they had about how to live. He even overruled those who forbade a wandering seeker who needed to talk to him.

A Secular Buddhist Spirituality

Ananda weeping at the Buddha's death[48]

At his death, a monk called, Anuruddha, Gotama's cousin and close friend, spoke spontaneously:

> "No movement of the breath, but with steadfast heart,
> Free from desires and tranquil — so the sage
> Comes to his end. By mortal pangs unshaken,
> His mind, like a flame extinguished, finds release."[49]

Anuruddha consoled the monks in their grief. But he also warned them about their plan for establishing a hierarchical system to guide the *sangha*, when their beloved Buddha had said they should simply follow the *dharma* and resist choosing a successor.

After His Death

The First Council[50]

After Gotama's cremation, a Council of Monks, all who had awakened, gathered to recite what they remembered of his teachings, gaining some consensus about what they should preserve. Thousands of thoughts and incidents were organised and memorised. Specific monks took responsibility for learning particular portions of the *buddha-vacana* ("the words of the Buddha") and the *buddha-sasana* (a broader concept, including stories and practices that illustrate, explain, or complement his teachings)[51]. Younger monks took up these torches so that the *dharma* fire could burn bright from generation to generation. These memories were transcribed on palm leaves three or four centuries after his death.

Many Buddhists are not content with a Buddha who awakened, taught Awakening, and then died. Was he not more significant than that? Do we not need his continued presence? Over the years, myths and legends were created to express a new kind of Buddha - a god-like figure who, some think, still lives as a conscious being. A more pragmatic Buddhism concentrates on his one life on earth and focuses on our present possibilities, not unseen worlds and unverifiable hopes.

Gotama was adamant that we should rely on his teachings, the *dharma*. He did not want us to be fixated on himself or a successor. He was not instigating a "cult of the personality", even though that is the way many of his followers present him. "Just follow the *dharma*" was his last advice.

It is rare to find representations of the Buddha that are not highly idealised. He is often depicted as the young Buddha, even before leaving the palace, at a time when he had not yet attained Awakening. He is commonly portrayed as maintaining the same physical vitality throughout his life. Yet, in his later years, he described himself as an old chariot held together by rags and vines. To go by the popular illustrations, he exemplified physical perfection, even in his final days. I doubt he would have endorsed such images – he was a great advocate of realism.

Over to You!

1. What impresses you most about the life of the Awakened Buddha?

2. Do you dare aspire to become a Buddha (fully Awake) yourself?

3. Have you ever faced an attack/temptation when you were moving towards greater positivity? If so, how do you interpret it?

Reflection: Balance

The Deer Park Instruction[52]

3.
Gotama's Middle Way (*majjhimapatipada*)

"The Middle Way refers to the Buddha's enlightened view of life and also the actions or attitudes that will create happiness for oneself and others. It is found in the ongoing, dynamic effort to apply Buddhist wisdom to the questions and challenges of life and society."
Soka Gakkai[53]

"The Middle Way is the idea that we make better judgments by avoiding fixed beliefs and being open to practical experience."
The Middle Way Society[54]

"The absoluteness of a claim depends on the person making it, their context and their mental state, not just on the words used in the claim. What makes absoluteness so unhelpful is not whether it is true or untrue, but that we are not in a position to check on absolutes or relate them to experience at all."
Robert M. Ellis[55]

Universal Truths to Live By

Gotama grasped the breadth and depth of human existence and discovered a way to inner peace and outward effectiveness. Reflecting on what he had learned from his own life and others, he realised how we can overcome suffering (stresses, pains, and dissatisfactions) and move towards a more satisfying and 'noble' life, through wisdom, ethics, and mind-training. Those prepared to examine their lives can improve them and even Awaken to their full potential and ultimate freedom.

But how would he present this life-changing discovery? We have the answer in the teaching preserved in a discourse titled, The First Turning of the *Dharma* Wheel (*Dhammacakkappavattana Sutta*). It is also known as the "Deer Park Sermon" because it was delivered in a deer park. This summarised his Awakening. Our Appendix contains a paraphrase of this crucial document. This document has served countless generations as a practical guide for spiritual self-development.

A Complex Simplicity

> "Everything should be made as simple as possible, but not simpler." Attributed to Albert Einstein

Gotama shared his insights in a way anyone could understand and use. He had no additional esoteric (hidden) teachings. Close to his death, he insisted, "I've held nothing back – I've not kept a closed fist."[56]

He had discovered many elements that promote liberation and many which obstruct it. Buddhism is famous for its many lists, reflecting the great variety within his experience and thus his teaching. To name only a few:

- Four Realities
- Four Tasks
- An Eightfold Path
- Twelve Steps
- Dependent Origination and Karma
- Five Mental Bundles
- Three Characteristics of Existence
- Six Perfections
- Five Hindrances

I think of them as facets of a diamond, different ways of illuminating the way to Awakening. Each has its own powerful insight, and we do not have to comprehend them all at once.

Gotama's message can seem overly complex and challenging. We can get lost in the details or overwhelmed by the depth of what he had to say. We might turn away from his good news for a simpler and less demanding gospel. But the complexity of Gotama's message and the realism of his demands are a pathway to our 'happiness' (in the fullest sense of the term).

Our approach is to apply this ancient teaching to our present-day context, exploring how each aspect might be reimagined and processed to relate to our situations. But we also explore how some more recent concepts and paradigms can complement Gotama's insights. The ultimate Awakening sees how all these 'sources of light' come together.

Some Will Understand

Through his Awakening, Gotama's understanding cut across his culture as much as it does ours. His vision included philosophical, ethical, and psychological insights about the way we think and act and their consequences. Just as in our time, many ignored the Buddha's message, while others dismissed it, failed to grasp it, or found it too threatening to pursue. But he came to realise that a significant number were ready to consider and embrace his teaching Those "with little dust in their eyes" could understand. What might seem impossibly rigorous to the majority will be seen as a path to freedom by others.

Gotama's approach acknowledges the many factors (involving thought, emotion, and action) that lead to Awakening. He knew of them, and of their benefits, from experience. He never asked of others anything that he had not tested himself.

Avoiding Extremes

The Awakened Gotama called his discovery the "Middle Way". He presented it in terms his former ascetic friends could understand, and in terms of his own experience:

> "You need to avoid two extremes. The first is an addiction to the pleasure of your senses. That will pull you away from your spiritual quest. It is the path of the world: ordinary, unprofitable, and unworthy. You've not gone forth from the householders' life for that! But there's another dangerous addiction, the devotion to self-mortification. It won't take you where you want to go either! It, too, is unprofitable, unnecessary, unworthy, and

painful. As you know, I've experienced both extremes and found neither helpful. Most importantly, I've discovered a different path that has borne fruit. I call it a Middle Way."[57]

During the first four decades of his life Gotama had committed himself to two different extremes. The first was self-indulgence ('Eat, drink, and be merry'). The second was extreme austerity ('Pleasure is the enemy of spirituality'). When he Awakened, he saw the need to follow a broader, more flexible path, applying a more measured approach while still adopting elements of the contrasting principles when necessary.

For example, his monks and nuns were required to live with few possessions. This recognised their commitment to full-time practice and their need to beg their daily meal. But he did not impose this minimalism on the householders who worked hard for themselves, their family and their community. Lay roles and responsibilities, so different from the monks and nuns, necessitated a greater openness to material goods.

Besides allowing us to see life with flexibility and openness to opinions other than our own, the Middle Way encourages us to avoid addictive, absolutist, and restrictive ideas that cloud our judgment and, all too often, lead to unfruitful confrontations. It is neither a compromise between opposing positions nor an averaging of opinions. It gives us the freedom and skilfulness to look with empathetic understanding for the positives in opinions we had rejected or hadn't even considered. In different circumstances we might share our understanding or encourage others to contribute.

The Buddha equated the Middle Way with the Eightfold Path. When he said this, he was not absolutizing those eight aims, but saying, in effect, 'Find what works for human advantage, and apply it skilfully'. We do well to use all eight – and any other positive practices and insights - towards Awakening. Few of us can master all at once!

The Benefits of Middle Way Thinking

Gautama's scepticism about the value of absolutes, if adopted today would free individuals and society at large from unhelpful extremes. A belief in irreconcilable differences will tend to cloud our thinking and bar us from many benefits. Approaching our own views with humility and being open to others' perspectives can lead to positive surprises and valuable redirections. In discussion and debate we can recognise and incorporate relevant insights from those who do not share our understanding.

As a boy I heard my father, a diplomat and academic who specialised in communications, explaining the difficulty of international negotiations with a cold-war example. 'In Russia the word 'compromise' has an overtone of unacceptable loss. When a Western adversary suggests they compromise, their Russian counterparts do not see it as coming to a mutually acceptable solution, but always with one winner and one loser.' Whether as career diplomats or in our own contexts, the Middle Way can free us from behaviours that, in the end, frustrate all involved.

In my late adolescence I maintained the unskilful position that finding a romantic partner would deliver all the missing ingredients in my life and put an end to all my emotional aches and pains. I longed for someone who would provide 'magic' or foolproof healing of all my insecurities and inadequacies. Even though I spent a lot of energy in my studies and subsequent employment I wasted much energy and put undue pressure on relationships that could not possibly meet my expectations.

As a result of all-or-nothing thinking while at University, I embraced the 'simple life' by giving away all my books, only to build up a library again within a year or two!

When I first embraced Buddhism, I began to reject all that I had thought was positive in Christianity, Islam, and other faiths. Now I'm comfortable in recognising skilfulness and wholesomeness in many faiths (and none) – while still drawing on the incredible benefits of Buddhist thought and practice.

An Ennobling Eightfold Path

Gotama concluded his affirmation of the Middle Way by declaring eight different emphases as the path to gain freedom from all suffering and its causes. This octet, used in harmony with one another, opens the way to Awakening:

> "And what is this Middle Way that I realised? It is an ennobling Eightfold Path (*ariya atthangika magga*) in which the eight together produce a vision and experiential knowledge that can calm our minds and emotions, permitting self-Awakening and freedom. Its emphases are:
>
> - Appropriate Perspective
> - Appropriate Resolve
> - Appropriate Speech

- Appropriate Action
- Appropriate Vocation
- Appropriate Effort
- Appropriate Mindfulness
- Appropriate Concentration.

Together, they release us from all that holds us back from Awakening."[58]

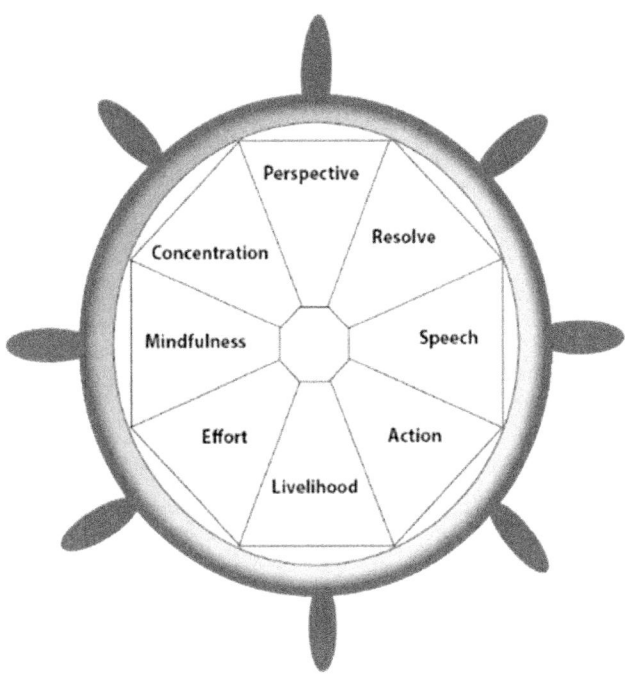

These eight emphases have come to be represented in a *Dharma* Wheel. Its contemporary depiction is as a helm (wheel) for steering a ship – underscoring that the Eightfold Path can be used to guide us on our way, as we discuss in Chapters Five to Ten.

A Medical Model

Many tell us that the Deer Park Sermon reflects a medical model. An article from the *Indian Journal of Endocrinology and Metabolism* (January-February 2021) states:

> "It is indeed a matter of supreme interest that the noble profession of medicine and the corpus of thought known as Buddhism are both concerned in their own way with the alleviation, control and ultimately the removal of human sufferings...
>
> "The Buddha's Four Noble Truths are a path toward healing, for in them lies the recognition of disease, its aetiology, its prognosis, and the remedy."

Perhaps drawing on a popular understanding of Jesus' work, many Western Buddhists, such as Norman Fischer, refer to Gotama as "The Great Physician" (see Lion's Roar, June 25, 2021). But Glenn Roberts, a retired consultant psychiatrist, offers a crucial clarification in a personal note he sent to me:

> "Ever since I came into contact with western Buddhist teachings, I was introduced to the idea that the Buddha was analogous to a 'doctor' and his core teaching to that of a medical process of engaging with suffering, identifying causes, offering a prognosis and embarking on a course of treatment.
>
> "I could see how that made sense. But as a doctor I also took issue with the appropriateness of the analogy. My difficulty was that medical practice is a process of meeting people with health problems, investigation, diagnosis and treatment ... in which the doctor plays a very active role in delivering health care and is responsible for the adequacy or not of his treatment.

"I don't think I ever heard or understood that the Buddha took such responsibilities with respect to his interactions with others nor did he 'treat' people. He was a teacher, and his teaching was all about how people could better understand their predicament and what action they could take, which they were responsible for themselves.

"It therefore seemed to me that rather than seeing the Buddha as some form of spiritual or philosophical doctor his activity as a teacher was much better matched to that of a healthcare educator or recovery coach."

Dr Glenn Roberts MD FRC Psych
Consultant Psychiatrist (Devon) retired

A Suitable Recovery

Recovery is a prime goal for our health services. Gotama's oft-quoted insistence that his main concern was "suffering and the end of suffering" makes sense in this context. But each of us needs to apply this teaching to our own particularities. The *dharma* is not a magic pill but rather a set of insights and practices. They will have little or no effect if they remain abstract principles. The transformative power comes from applying his insights. It is for us to figure out how to apply them and then take appropriate action.

In Buddhism, one size and shape will not fit all. We might ask, 'How did the Buddha think and live?' But that is just a powerful beginning to finding the answer for ourselves.

One important aspect of our openness to *dharma*-based development is the language we use to understand its challenging message. Even in translation, its ancient Indian forms can hinder our reception of Gotama's radical instructions and prevent a realistic response. It is important to sense the vitality and impact of the original teachings.

Over to You!

1. Are there any specific extremes that you need to avoid in following a 'Middle Way'?

2. Would your relationships be improved if you adopted a Middle Way approach? If so, how?

3. Do you welcome a philosophy/spirituality/way of life that demands your commitment to experience the benefits?

CONTENTMENT HERE AND NOW

A Secular Buddhist Spirituality

Reflection: An Uncertain Journey

The Tian Tan "Big Buddha"[59]

NB: The swastika is a Buddhist symbol of peace and harmony, predating its Nazi use by more than two millennia.

4.
Gotama's Twelve-Step Programme

"Buddhism is neither pessimistic nor optimistic. If anything at all, it is realistic, for it takes a realistic view of life and the world. It looks at things objectively (*yathābhūtam*). It does not falsely lull you into living in a fool's paradise, nor does it frighten and agonise you with all kinds of imaginary fears and sins. It tells you exactly and objectively what you are and what the world around you is, and shows you the way to perfect freedom, peace, tranquillity and happiness."
Walpola Rahula[60]

"If asked to list in propositional form their four most considered convictions about life, most people would probably stammer. The Four Noble Truths constitute Buddha's answer to that request. Together they stand as the axioms of his system, the postulates from which the rest of his teachings logically derive."
Vinaire[61]

The Four Ennobling Realities
(cattāri ariyasaccāni)

From the broad perspective of the Middle Way with its eight emphases, the Buddha turned to four key insights. As we realise their implications and react intelligently (skilfully) to these realities, the frustrations of ordinary living are transformed. When we discover their relevance, they register in our bodies, minds, and emotions and then in our decisions and actions. This is the path to contentment.

Traditionally, *cattāri ariyasaccāni* is translated as "the four noble truths", but this can distort our understanding. With the scholar Peter Harvey, I prefer "reality" (or "fact") to "truth". The Buddha talks about our raw life experiences and how we might best process them. All four are facts of life we must engage with entirely if we are to awaken to the best our lives can offer. Sadly, people often favour unhelpful unrealities to the 'hard truths' of the *dharma*.

Rather than calling them 'noble' realities, I prefer 'ennobling'. Gotama confronts us with these four facts because they will permanently transform us if we respond intelligently. They contribute to our spiritual 'nobility'. The original word for noble (*ariya*) can mean "not ordinary", "valuable", "precious", "pure", and "rich". Spiritual Awakening contains all these qualities. As we progressively come alive to this possibility, we'll want to change whatever threatens our true well-being, if and as we overcome our fear of changing our mind and actions.

Reality #1:
We Begin with Our Need

The first fact is ***dukkha (suffering, pain, stress)***, the reality of our discomfort and discontent, prompted by the inevitable pain and stress of living as imperfect people in an imperfect world. Even those "with everything" are not immune. Gotama identified four universal sufferings: birth, ageing, sickness, and death. We come into an imperfect world as imperfect people. Various *suttas* describe his quest for enlightenment as motivated by a desire to find a solution to these four.

Gotama didn't say that life is total misery. But he saw how our reactions to life experiences can and do cause suffering. Some is inescapable, but much is self-generated. The death of my parents and my son John brought with it an inevitable, complex sense of loss. To Gotama's four universal sufferings we might add our own: family life, work life, relationships. Again, they do not bring uninterrupted pain and discontent. But neither are they without those experiences (*dukkha*). He expanded his description of *dukkha*: being stuck with what we dislike, not getting what we want, and fearing losing what we have all add to the pain of our existence.[62] Each of us will have our own, unique list.

As a prison chaplain, I learned that most prisoners have had adverse childhood experiences. Perhaps most of us have. These can profoundly affect our emotions, thoughts and behaviours without our realising the source. Our lives can be satisfactory in our conscious experience ("nothing to complain about"), but with a vague, half-realised sense of violation or deprivation below the surface of our awareness.

We can be driven by an underlying sense of anxiety or discouragement – whether about our specific situations, a sense of chaos and uncertainty, or a deep loneliness. The songs "What's it all about, Alfie?" (Burt Bacharach) and "Is that all there is?" (Jerry Leiber & Mike Stoller) were modern 'classics' because they spoke to the depths within so many. They certainly resonated with my young adult consciousness and my emotions.

We can be thankful for our *dukkha*, because it motivates us to seek a better life.

Reality #2:
The Cause of All Unnecessary Pain

Fact two, **samudaya (arising)**, is that our dissatisfactions and distortions are often self-generated. When I cut deep into my thumb with a circular saw, the cause of the pain indeed came from outside myself. But my suffering sprung from the way I responded to it. I worried that I'd lose the thumb (which I didn't); I feared painful stitching (soon forgotten); for several weeks I was anxious whether my boss would dismiss me from my summer job (he didn't). What a wasted use of my energies and emotions! If you can distinguish your self-generated distress about an experience or situation from the actual event, you've grasped the second fact.

Our reactive responses are not just about such concerns. They include inappropriate or imbalanced attractions and hostility. Perhaps the most difficult to identify is the way we base so many responses on ignorance and delusion (a lack of knowledge or resistance to the facts)[63].

You might question this reality because it is so clear that some unwelcome experiences are not self-generated. We all can recall times when we faced great disappointments that were not in any way our fault. Yet we are still responsible for our consequent and perhaps continuous suffering because of our own reactivity to such occurrences. The sharpest pains in our lives are, most often, those we generate within ourselves. These come from the unhelpful ways we process our difficulties and disappointments, whatever their source. The Buddha's analysis is stated in the "Discourse On Causes" (*Nidana Sutta*), traditionally known as "the three poisons":

> "Monks, these three are causes for the origination of actions. **Greed** is a cause for the origination of actions. **Aversion** is a cause for the origination of actions. **Delusion** is a cause for the origination of actions."

The open secret of the Buddha's contentedness lies in how he processed events. When his cousin opposed him, his close disciples left him, and his followers disappointed him Gotama responded with equanimity - without the reactionary behaviours that can easily complicate our lives.

Gotama came to realise the possibility of a radically different approach to our suffering and stress from an unhelpful reactivity. And he had discovered a better way, by responding to our pain with skilfulness. Thus, the next reality.

Reality #3:
Reason to be Hopeful - Suffering is Optional

Fact three, **nirodha** (**ending**), is that our suffering can cease. We need not be victims of our reactivity! We can counter and control it. This possibility is presented in the myth of what Gotama experienced at the cusp of his Awakening. Mara (the Buddhist devil) tried to shift Gotama's focus with violent threats, then with eroticism. But the Buddha-to-be would not be deterred.

An effective mental mantra is "Pain is inevitable, but suffering is optional." It has often been called a 'Buddhist proverb'. It is a modern, not ancient, expression. Yet, the meaning expresses the Buddha's teaching and the traditions that emerged from it. In "How a Fake Buddha Quote Completely Changed My Life", Braden Wong shares the effect of a terrible hip injury and his learning that suffering is an optional mental function he could abandon:

> "The pain constantly clicking at the joint, while others told me to "suck it up", pushed me to the limit until I snapped. I cried for surgery - even if it was irreversible, I didn't care. I was broken. Fortunately, the surgery never came. Instead, surfing the internet one day, I stumbled upon a rather peculiar quote: '…suffering is optional'. The attribution to Buddha was completely incorrect… But it didn't matter. This Buddhist advice changed my life forever. My hip pain is now a source of gratitude — though it still occasionally hurts. I now know that had I not been injured, I would have never cared for fitness, developed a productive daily routine, or strong personal systems. Had I not been mentally broken, I would have

never developed the mental strength needed for later battles."[64]

I first experienced the great distinction between pain and suffering when I injured my lower back while delivering a trunkful of blood to a hospital during a summer job driving a taxi. It is still affecting me over 50 years later. I'd never known such pain as when my lower disc tore apart. But soon after the injury, I began to laugh with joy and amusement. The day before, I had been privileged with a vivid sense of the goodness of life. It seemed that love filled every crack and cranny of the universe. When love is everywhere, what reason had I to feel sorry for myself?

The more significant application of our liberation from a fixation on the unwelcome aspects of life is emotional rather than physical. *Dharmic* realism has countered and conquered my own sense of isolation and rejection that has haunted me for decades. It was embedded in my earliest memory and reinforced in my childhood. By learning to view it realistically, I have found freedom from its painful effects. This emotion sometimes surfaces from a hidden part of me. When this happens, I greet it as the childish confusion that it is and contradict its discouraging message as required.

Reality #4:
A Concrete Way Forward

The final fact is that there is a positive path (*magga*) that leads to a permanent release from our reactivity. As we've seen, this is the Middle Way, the culmination of what Gotama learned and taught. It consists of eight different practices. These eight have been grouped into three main clusters:

-Wisdom (Perspective and Resolve)
-Ethics (Speech, Action, and Vocation) and
-Mind Training (Effort, Mindfulness, and Concentration).

Although Gotama began with the wisdom paths, many start their journey into Buddhism with his three ethical paths or with a meditation practice. With Buddhism, it does not matter where we start. What's important is to keep going deeper and broader, towards Awakening.

An Example of Eliminating Unnecessary Suffering

An example may help clarify how we benefit from Gotama's approach. A well-embedded sense of social alienation has kept me from wholesome participation with others. At parties, my gut feeling can be articulated as, "They're enjoying one another – but there's no place here for me." Or I could be defensively judgmental, "How superficial! - Just small talk and laughter."

When I sense this kind of reactivity, I now correct it (sometimes consciously, sometimes spontaneously). This is so much better than my discomfort with social gatherings. I remind myself that I enjoy getting to know people; this motivates me to converse with others in the room.

I am constantly discovering that no one is uninteresting when you probe beyond surface superficialities! I now enjoy these mutual interchanges. When someone clarifies that they do not want a conversation with me, I remind myself that rapport requires a mutual interest or parallel experience. If it's absent with someone, I'll find it with another. When someone isn't interested in me, it's no big deal! Through an awareness of the possibility of self-generated discomfort I can nip it in the bud. As well, the skills of the Eightfold Path help my positive interactions with others. I'm still not a party animal, but the *dharma* has helped me enjoy most social situations.

Four Tasks

Gotama's Awakening came when he realised that: "[his] stress was **comprehended**… its origin was **abandoned**… its cessation was directly **experienced**… The Eightfold Path was **developed**." [65]

These are the Four Tasks to be embraced by those who seek Awakening. They spring from a realisation that the Four Realities are meant to prompt action, not just agreement. They demand a fulsome response if we are to improve our lives.

Stephen Batchelor has presented the Gotama's Four Tasks as ELSA[66]: **Embrace** life as it is, including its inevitable difficulties; **Let go** of your instinctive reactivity to discomforting situations and events; **See** your reactive actions reduce and disappear; and **Act** in a way that implements each of the eight ways leading to contentment.

Peter Harvey writes of a similar pattern. "The four true realities taught by the Buddha are not as such things to "believe" but to (a) accept (b) see and (c) contemplate, and (d) respond to appropriately: (1) by fully **understanding** *dukkha*/pain/the painful, (2) **abandoning** that which originates it, (3) personally **experiencing** its cessation and (4) **cultivating** the path that leads to this."[67]

Harvey's insight emphasises the dimension of continuance to the model. Once we experience the benefits of following Gotama's wise advice, we must keep cultivating the factors that bring contentment into our lives, or we will lose it. Over time, with practice, skilful thoughts and actions become a natural part of our lives. However, the fact of Impermanence spotlights a need for continuing awareness and, when needed, conscious application.

Twelve-Steps

A Twelve Step Programme is implied within Gotama's teaching in the "First Turning of the *Dharma* Wheel" *Sutta*.

> "Until I understood the necessity of each of these Twelve Steps – applying all three phases to each of the four realities – I could not claim to have discovered a full, supreme Awakening. But when I experienced how things really are, in all Twelve Steps… I knew that my heart's deliverance was unassailable." [A paraphrase of this *sutta* is contained in the Appendix.]

We should not confuse these twelve with the Twelve Step Programme of Alcoholics Anonymous (AA), and its many derivatives.[68]

To summarise, Gotama's twelve-step programme applies each of the Four Realities in three phases.

First, we **Grasp** how each reality relates to our human condition; we understand Gotama's basic point. Then we **Apply** it to ourselves. Finally, we **Realise** the benefits of our response, experiencing its benefits.[69] With all these phases applied to all the realities we can speak of twelve steps towards completing the journey to Awakening. It might be expressed in the formula:

4 Realities x 3 Phases = 12 Steps

These twelve steps, or *dharma* applications move us forward in our spiritual journey and are all necessary for our Awakening.

As we progress through the phases of each of the realities, we will see our suffering for what it is (Steps 1, 2, 3), understand how we ourselves generate so much unnecessary suffering (Steps 4, 5, 6), experience the release of this suffering (Step 7, 8, 9), and live according to the Eightfold Path (Steps 10, 11, 12).

Gotama presents his Four Realities in a logical sequence, which might imply an orderly progression of realisations and actions. But our life experience is often not a series of orderly steps - but more a uniquely ordered journey. Thus, these Twelve Steps are not so much a map as a checklist. However, one way or another, our journey is not complete until it includes all twelve.

Gotama's Twelve Step Programme

Ennobling Reality #4 *there is a* positive pathway (*magga*) out of *dukkha*	Phase 3: Live it Phase 2: Try it Phase 1: Understand it	Step 12 Step 11 Step 10
Ennobling Reality #3 *nirodha* - our suffering of *dukkha* can end	Phase 3: Live it Phase 2: Try it Phase 1: Understand it	Step 9 Step 8 Step 7
Ennobling Reality #2 *samudaya* - we generate our *dukkha*	Phase 3: Live it Phase 2: Try it Phase 1: Understand it	Step 6 Step 5 Step 4
Ennobling Reality #1 *dukkha* exists	Phase 3: Live it Phase 2: Try it Phase 1: Understand it	Step 3 Step 2 Step 1

12 Steps (not necessarily linear)

Diagram produced by Brian Duffy (editor)

First, we understand some aspect of Gotama's teaching. Grasping any *dharma* 'truth' is crucial, but insufficient if we do not move from generalised, abstract thought to a more vivid awareness of how it affects our moment-by-moment existence. We need to relate it to our unique personal dynamics, histories, personalities, and psychologies.

Then we start to apply it to ourselves and see what effect that has. Merely affirming the Four Realities will not shift our lives from discontent to contentment. Full awakening comes after the steps are applied over time as part of our conscious behaviour. Gotama intended to show us that nothing less than "direct experience" will awaken us. None of the Four Realities would have their intended impact if simply accepted as valid principles. We must apply them to our personalities and situations.

Finally, the teaching becomes embedded within us. When it is expressed without conscious application; it becomes an ingrained habit, and it can become a life-long trait.

Such a three-fold progression through each Reality may well be implied when the *Lotus Sutra* declared the *dharma* was "good in the beginning, good in the middle, and good at the end." [70] It can be good for us too, if (and only if) we follow it.

Although each of the Twelve Steps can be immensely challenging, they are all achievable.

Good News for All Who Live It

It's too easy to think of the Buddha's enlightenment as coming to him in a moment of inspiration and his transformation happening as quickly as it takes to say "abracadabra" or to wave a magic wand. But the fact is that Gotama's full Awakening took a great amount of energy and time. He had prepared for many years before his great breakthrough. Then, in an evening's meditation, he saw it all come together in a complex simplicity. He devoted the rest of his life to encouraging the same seriousness from all of his followers, whether monks or laity.

He has presented a practical, proven formula for our spiritual development. Our continuing growth transforms well-established habits and deeply entrenched behaviours. The goal may seem unobtainable by ordinary efforts. But we can draw upon resources of which we are not consciously aware, as we discuss in later chapters.

Gotama's original offer was intended for all – ordained and non-ordained – and still is. When he spoke of "four assemblies" (ordained men and women, male and female householders), he was making it clear that anyone who followed his teaching could experience what he experienced.

At the end of his life, the Buddha mentioned his equal respect for people from all four assemblies to awaken:

> "I won't die until my monks and nuns, laymen and laywomen, show themselves to be true disciples: wise, well-disciplined, able and learned, preservers of the *dharma* in their teaching and example. Each must demonstrate that they have learned my teaching so thoroughly that they can teach it, preach it, proclaim it, establish it, explain it in detail and make it clear. When contrary opinions arise, they need to be able to counter them thoroughly with this convincing and liberating *dharma*."[71]

The Awakened life is not beyond the capacity of any of us!

Over to You!

1. What stresses, pains, or dissatisfactions do you most want to eradicate or reduce in your life? Are you willing to develop an eightfold skilfulness or follow Gotama's twelve step journey to do so?

2. Does Gotama's analysis of our common existential 'problem' (*dukkha*) and the path towards contentment (*sukha*) connect with your self-understanding?

3. Would you describe the Four Ennobling Realities as optimistic or pessimistic? As empowering or discouraging?

CONTENTMENT HERE AND NOW

Reflection: Intrusion

Buddha Head, with "Third (wisdom) Eye"[72]

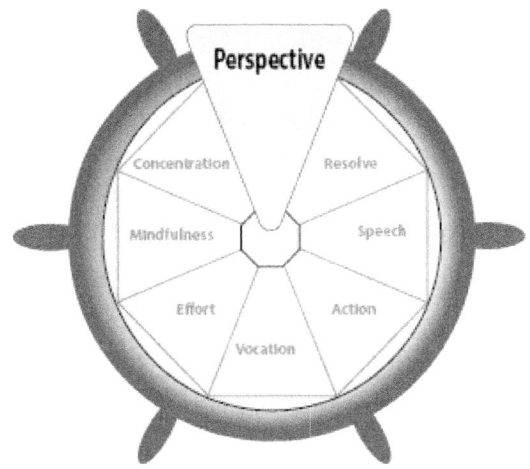

5.
Appropriate Perspective
(samma ditthi)

"I've often said I wish that people could realise their dreams of wealth and fame so that they could see that is not where you are going to find your sense of completion." Jim Carrey[73]

"It is not wisdom if we simply believe what we are told. True wisdom is to directly see and understand for ourselves." (unnamed author) Buddhanet[74]

What's 'Appropriate'?

Each aspect of the Eightfold Path is modified by *samma*, traditionally translated as "right" and even "perfect". This leads some to accept a rules-based *dharma* of rights and wrongs and some to strive for a toxic perfectionism. The root meaning of *samma* is "connected", implying "a helpful and realistic engagement".[75] Using the term appropriate with each aspect of the path reflects Gotama's understanding in a more empowering way. It's appropriate to connect broad principles to the complexities and constraints of each situation. For example, the Awakened Gotama did not counter absolute rulers directly – a suicidal approach in his day. But he often found a subtler way of influencing them, by inviting them to draw their own conclusions (informed by his perspectives).

Wisdom

The Eightfold Path towards our ultimate freedom and contentment begins with two aspects now commonly grouped as Wisdom: Appropriate Perspective and Appropriate Resolve. But what is wisdom? It is seeing ourselves and the world we live in realistically and responding accordingly. When we can see correctly, we can take appropriate actions. But if we are blind to reality, we are left to stumble in the dark.

Prajna is the original Pali word for wisdom, its root meaning is "insight" or "intuitive knowledge".[76] This implies something more than rational knowledge. Wisdom implies an experiential and emotional dimension that is much more than factual, rational knowledge. Wise old men and women have lived long enough to see for themselves the danger of infidelity, unrestrained anger, a life committed to career advancement and little else. Such wisdom may be gained by examining our own life stories from the perspective of lessons learned. But wise perspectives can come from careful observation of others as well. The wisdom that contributed to Gotama's Awakening was based on considering his own life and observing others.[77]

Before I was helped to "see" my life more realistically I often felt a sense of primal rejection in many social situations, and I doubted the sincerity of those expressing approval. Once my view of life became more aligned with the actuality of my social environment (and intimate relationships), my experience changed immeasurably, and an immense burden was lifted. As Thich Nhat Hanh has said, "Unless and until we're able to face our suffering, we can't be present and available to life, and happiness will continue to elude us."[78]

There is much benefit from re-viewing our lives in light of *dharma* understandings, such as the Four Realities. We can consider the essence of "right view" in terms of these four.

> "And what is right view? Knowledge about stress, the origination of stress, the cessation of stress, and the way of practice leading to the cessation of stress." *Mahasatipatthana Sutta*, (The Longer Discourse on Mindfulness Meditation).

Soi Sage!

I'm told that French parents guide their children towards appropriate behaviour with the phrase Soi sage! (Be wise!).

That contrasts with Mom and Dad's Be good! Both these phrases probably stem from cultural and parental norms and suggest, 'Behave like I'm telling you to!'. Little children may need such guidance, but it is inappropriate for adults. Vishen Lakhiani calls these external requirements "brules" ("bullsh!t rules").[79] We start out with unreasoning obedience to parental and social norms. But we can grow up to make choices for ourselves. Buddhists are encouraged to replace "being good" and "doing the right thing" with "being skilful" and "doing what is wise".

Gotama's approach is more nuanced than a set of rules for living. He gave us insightful principles for changes that we decide for ourselves. Both wisdom elements, with the other six aspects of his Path, are the compass and map for our journey to Awakening. As a young adult, he saw the need for something different from what his family and society expected of him. Thus, we speak of his "going forth" and "renunciation". He was out of sync with what we've been taught as 'realistic'.

Typically, faith traditions distinguish between 'worldly' (mundane) wisdom and 'spiritual' wisdom. But thinking of two separate worlds (earthly and heavenly) is not helpful. Instead, we seek spiritual reality within our mundane existence – a matter of perception, not place. This is analogous to the counter-intuitive understanding of quantum physics that a phenomenon can be viewed as material and energy – coexisting yet seeming to follow different laws.

Gotama spoke of distinct stages of Awakening. We usually start with learning to live more skilfully in the world, which is appropriate to beginning *dharma* farers. Eventually, we radically revise our understanding and develop an empowering perspective on life (thanks to the same *dharma*). Finally we are ready to "cross the stream" (Gotama's phrase for living the Awakened life) led by values, intuitions, rational reasoning, and behaviours that contrast with 'worldly' assumptions and methods. Our Awakening proves to be an increasingly meaningful and contented life. Awakening seems a world away from the popular understanding of 'happiness'. Yet it is lived out in the world into which we were born. This is similar to Jesus' emphasis that the 'kingdom of heaven is within you' (not in a land beyond earth's atmosphere, never reached until after we die.)[80]

Understanding Causation

Understanding causation is at the heart of Gotama's thinking. If there was any one factor in Gotama's opening the door to Awakening, it was when the penny dropped about causation:

> "With unfailing clarity, I reviewed how people change. The results are different - inferior and superior, fair and ugly, fortunate and unfortunate - according to people's actions, talk, and thoughts. Some conduct themselves unskilfully. They put down admirable folk. They hold useless opinions. The result is deprivation, spiritual ruin, and even hellish anguish. But those who conducted themselves nobly – with helpful opinions, respect for those who deserve it, and helpful actions – improve. They end up in a good place, with better dispositions."[81]

This paraphrase omits Gotama's mention of death and rebirth, which does not feature in our secular approach, though it was a widespread assumption in ancient India. Gotama warned against focusing on a life other than our present one.[82] Every moment that follows the next is a time of rebirth (rebecoming). Certainly, there are some apparent advantages to continuity. But the greater insight is that we change, for better or worse, with our thoughts, words, and actions. "Rebirth" happens every moment of our lives, often with habitual thoughts and activities which we take for an unchanging personality. As we reaffirm a thought or action, it is strengthened (changed).

Gotama's understanding of causation has been called 'the Buddha's theory of everything'.[83] He saw it as an inescapable and universal phenomenon and a key to Awakening. It was simplified into a formula: "This being, that becomes. From the arising of this, that arises. From the ceasing of this, that ceases."[84] All phenomena have a causal connection, even if we cannot calculate exactly what it is.

Karma is a Sanskrit word meaning "action" The wisdom of *karma* is that all our intentional actions (even mental ones) have consequences for us; we cannot stop them from bearing sweet or bitter fruit. Sometimes these consequences are obvious and predictable, but often not. No one can see immediately the subtle character changes or all the benefits and harm that we contribute to.

Karma is a natural process, sometimes mysterious, and never fully predictable. As we act skilfully (with wisdom and love), other people will tend to respond more favourably to us, as well as our developing some expansions and enrichments to our inner life. However, it is over-simplistic to promise specific results for specific actions. Life is too complex for that.

Karmic consequences reflect a natural process, sometimes mysterious, and never fully predictable. They do not lend themselves to simplistic formulas. Our actions can alienate us from or endear us to those on the receiving end, whatever our motivation and attitude. Bad things happen to good people (and vice versa). Thus, *karma* is never fully predictable.

Some people use this concept to warn, scare, or manipulate others. I have seen a booklet to explain *karma*, advising that those who supported the nuns and monks would receive a 'good' rebirth. Those who were not generous would experience poverty in their future life. If you slandered others, it said, you'd be reborn with a cleft pallet! Gotama saw *karma*'s positive implications, but not primarily in terms of rebirth rewards and punishments.

Karma spotlights individual actions and their consequences. This is useful because our intended actions, over time, do change our character and often return in positive or negative experiences. Yet, it requires a broader perspective.

The fact is some genetic, sociological, cultural, and other factors, remain at present unexplainable. As much as I try to take responsibility for my actions, I realise that they are under the influence of others. Although I never knew either my maternal or paternal grandparents, they have influenced me through their genetics and their influence on my parents. "Society" and the many groups and individuals that have helped to shape my thoughts, habits, and expectations are beyond calculation.

I can name people who contributed greatly to my development. Many individuals and groups played a crucial role in shaping my understanding of myself and the world. As a parent and educator, I've been influenced by my children, my students, and my peers as much as those who raised and educated me.

Individualised *karma* is an important but partial understanding of causation. The greater principle, more central to Gotama's understanding and personal Awakening, is dependent origination (*paticca-samupplada*). This concept provides a subtler and more complex causal analysis. It rests on the insight or intuition that we are influenced by genetics and by many other influences from childhood onwards. The so-called 'great man' theory, which explains world history as the consequence of single individuals, is naïve and inaccurate.

> "You must admit that the genesis of a great man depends on the long series of complex influences which have produced the race in which he appears and the social state into which that race has slowly grown. Before he can remake his society, his society must make him."[85]

Indra's Net

Early Buddhism borrowed from Vedic teaching the figure of Indra's Net. Indra was a major god in the ancient Indian pantheon. He wove a vast jewelled net, with each jewel representing a member of humanity. Each reflected all the others. We all 'inter-are', to use the language of Thich Nhat Hanh. Nothing and no one exist in isolation and self-sufficiency; everything "inter-is", part of the whole.

You could demonstrate dependent origination and interbeing by doing a mind map of one significant action you initiated. Note all the factors that permitted and influenced it, from the big bang that began our universe to the present. Include evolution, heredity, culture, economics, and the contributions of unseen providers, such as the gas that kept you warm, the water that sustained your life and whatever contributed to your being from early childhood onwards. The point is that our actions are not as independent as we often believe them to be.

Realistic Uncertainty, Calculated Positivity

An oft-told story, originating in Chinese Buddhism, tells of an impoverished elderly farmer and son who scratched out a marginal living from their small farm. Their vulnerability led a neighbour to check up on them with a weekly visit.

The neighbour always greeted the friend, asking, "What's new?"

On one visit, the old man replied, "Last night, our horse ran off."

"That's terrible", said the neighbour.

The old man replied, "Maybe good. Maybe bad. Who can tell?"

A week later, the neighbour appeared with his usual, "What's new?"

"My son went to look for our horse and found him with a herd of wild ones. He managed to bring it back with three more. He's taming them now."

"How wonderful" his neighbour exclaimed.

"Maybe good. Maybe bad. Who can tell?" the farmer replied.

The following week, the same question. The farmer replied, "My son broke his leg while training the horses."

"So sad. So sorry."

"Might be good. Might be bad. Who can tell?"

The story progresses with a military gang visiting the farm looking for able-bodied men. His son was in no shape to be conscripted. "How fortunate you both are", the neighbour judged – with the usual response from the old man.

We cannot know the consequences of specific events and actions. Yet it is easy to calculate our circumstance (or another person's situation) as though we could. Few urges are as powerful as the desire for certainty. It brings simplicity to the unavoidable, often unwelcome complications of life. Gotama recognised this complexity. But he also saw recurring patterns that allow us to commit to a programme of positive change that will take us to full Awakening.

Contentment is possible! This is the thrust of Gotama's unfailingly positive but relentlessly realistic philosophy. While we cannot control all that will happen, we can alter our unskilful reactivity. This philosophy has been characterised as melioristic (aiming at getting better) and pragmatic. It orients us to expect that life can improve through our efforts. This conviction is needed in the face of the multi-crisis we are facing. Beyond our well-being, our good deeds and thoughts may have beneficial effects in many ways we will never know.

The Deathless

"The Deathless" (*Amata*) is a concept that Gotama often used as his final discovery's goal. We might think of it as The Eternal, in the mystical present tense of the awakened perception. It is not unknown to Christian mysticism, and is described in the beginning lines of William Blake's *Auguries of Innocence*[86]:

> To see a World in a Grain of Sand
> And a Heaven in a Wild Flower
> Hold Infinity in the palm of your hand
> And Eternity in an hour

Gotama was not alluding to a heavenly afterlife, similar to Islam and Christianity, but the ultimate perspective of altered consciousness in which all is seen as one, and all tensions between 'subject' and 'object' are removed. We know that he did not affirm an everlasting Creator/Judge and that he considered the Indian gods (*deva*s) as enjoying only a temporary existence. He never promised eternal life to anyone, despite its obvious appeal. Rather, his perspective was to realise our potential of seeing the life we are living here and now as it really is a unified field.

We might think of lofty concepts (for example, generosity) as deathless (eternal and invariable). Yet when we embrace them, they become touched by our humanity and become impermanent. We compound and condition them by our engagement, which adds a developing, shifting aspect to their experience. The ultimate Buddhist goal (Awakening) is not found in fixed interpretations of our values, but in relating them towards universal benefit, according to the circumstances before us. The goal is not an abstract perfection, but something much more realistic and achievable. A wise understanding keeps this as an ongoing perspective.

Three Characteristics of Existence

Another crucial perspective for realistic living is Gotama's intuition of the Three Characteristics of Existence (*tri-lakshana*), namely, (1) Impermanence, (2) No Self ("no fixed self"), and (3) Dissatisfaction. Understanding them is key to accepting life as we invariably experience it.

(1.) *Anicca* is a Pali word that means "unstable", "impermanent", and "inconstant". Thus, it affirms that everything is changing. Everything exists as a process, in transition, and thus not a stable entity.

Nothing wholly disappears, but everything changes. We know that all the material in the universe is made from atoms, and that no atom is static. The same principle of movement applies to our social structures and our individual thoughts and emotions, and even our values (in their applications and implications).

(2.) No-self (*anatta*) affirms the consequence of impermanence as it applies to all phenomena, including ourselves (our 'self' or 'soul'). Nothing in us, or anything else, has a fixed, permanent nature.

Think of a leaf. It is a process from bud to mulch. Every aspect of our humanity is similarly fluid and unfixed – irretrievably 'porous' and dynamic. Are you the same as your infant or adolescent self? Neither am I! But there's something in us that wants to think we have an unalterable essence. Through deep meditation and reflection, we can realise the fluidity of our consciousness (our minds) and all else that we often assume is unalterable.

Considering the universality and ultimacy of Impermanence, we will see that our "self" (often termed a soul) cannot and does not exist as a permanent entity. This realisation enhances our freedom and emboldens our expectations of positive change. The opposite can tie us down and prevent self-development. Two "fetters" (constraining our spiritual growth) are a longing for material and immaterial existence. Better to experience life as it comes (and goes).

(3.) Dissatisfaction (*dukkha*) is a universal characteristic of constant change. We can easily experience Impermanence and Insubstantiality in a painful and distressing way. But this inescapable aspect of our lives can be accepted with equanimity and used to counter our reactivity, promote healthy responses and other positive actions.

The assertion of these three characteristics of existence is not a metaphysical statement so much as an experiential one. When we realise that nothing is unchanging and of a fixed nature, we realise that we cannot depend on unchanging realities for our security. But we can respond constructively and thus discover a deep contentment.

Spiritual Evolution

The idea of spiritual evolution also helped me recognise the potential of imitating the Buddha's way of being. As civilised human beings we do not need to live by the laws of the jungle. Our species has emerged from the jungle and established a more complex environment with new possibilities. We are developing a different kind of power (a 'softer' more subtle power, not just brute strength) and different skillsets to promote a more comprehensive concept of a secure and well-provided life. This possibility of flourishing rather than merely surviving has a spiritual dimension. I can see a universal, tolerant, wise and compassionate humanity emerging with increasing strength, from the 18th Century onwards.

This new spirituality is becoming popular and empowering. The possibility of living like a Buddha fits within this wider context.[87]

A secular understanding of spirituality includes the concept of improving our human nature, to the advantage of ourselves and others. We can consider it an aspect of wisdom and a way of interpreting the *dharma*. The concept of evolution was not known to Gotama. Yet it is a helpful hypothesis for understanding our place in the evolving 'river of life'.

We can extend the principle of evolution (the survival of characteristics that are best suited to the environment) to the spiritual realm. Many of us develop spiritually because it makes us more positive, more constructive, and thus better able to cope with life's many stresses and challenges.

A Secular Buddhist Spirituality

The "spiritual" dimension of our lives cannot be seen, measured, weighed, smelled, or tasted; it is beyond the reach of our five senses. However, we can "sense" its reality with our intuitions and emotions. Most important, we can develop our spirituality to make us more able to experience the fullest, deepest kind of contentment, which makes for better living. A crucial factor is gaining the wisest, most reliable perspectives about human nature, its possibilities, and the means of achieving them.

Exploring spirituality since my adolescence and exposing myself to a wide variety of religious and secular approaches, I have found the *dharma* offers a most credible reading of the human experience. It also presented me with a wide variety of practices – many of which I'll be introducing in later chapters – from which to develop a pattern that fitted my personality and was conducive to my spiritual development. Since Buddhism is an experience-based philosophy or 'faith' that does not claim to be a revelation from another world, I could test every thought and practice and find what was appropriate to me. As with Gotama's advice to the Kalamas, we are encouraged to do the same.

Writing for the Royal College of Psychiatrists, Dr Maya Spencer presents an understanding of spirituality that sits well with a non-theistic and secular Buddhism:

> "Spirituality involves the recognition of a feeling or sense or belief that there is something greater than myself, something more to being human than sensory experience, and that the greater whole of which we are part is cosmic or divine in nature. Spirituality means knowing that our lives have significance in a context beyond a mundane everyday existence at the level of biological needs that

drive selfishness and aggression. It means knowing that we are a significant part of a purposeful unfolding of Life in our universe."[88]

"Selfishness and aggression" (in the quote above) relate to Gotama's concepts of grasping and hate. We can also mention lust (sexual desire). These are part of our animal inheritance, reinforced by their advantages in the development of our species. We cannot escape the urges and inclinations, which are often present in our immediate reactivity to perceived threats and enhancements. But, Gotama taught they need not be the final word. With Awakening, we are aware of their presence, but also of our ability to respond differently, according to *dharmic* principles. This freedom allows us to respond skilfully, develop our character, and experience beneficial *karma*.

Psychologist-philosopher Karl Jaspers introduced the concept of an "Axial Age" (between 800 and 500 BCE) in which humanity in many different contexts experienced a maturing of their spiritual sense. Many great adepts (including Gotama, Socrates, Confucius, Lau-Tzu, Isaiah, and Zarathustra) initiated profound changes in human understanding of their place in the universe and society. This shifted humanity's religious sensitivity towards a more ethical understanding and a greater responsibility for their thoughts and actions. More recently, another spiritual emphasis, from many quarters, is minimising the direct actions of the supernatural and emphasising human autonomy. This has led to a rich and varied secular humanism, supported by Albert Einstein and non-religious Buddhism.

Ineffability

It is crucial to realise that the *dharma* points us to an experience of "ultimate reality", which remains beyond representation. No teaching can reveal this sense of "direct experience". We are finite, and the universe is not. Our senses are limited and cannot fully embrace its vast complexity. But this does not keep us from Awakening to some sense of a comprehensive and ultimate reality or a sense of its presence in specific events and objects. This "mystical" intuition is beyond any representation – though many use code words for it, such as "the All", "God", and Gotama's favourite, the "deathless". The *dharma* offers "84,000" concepts to help us approach it. This includes ideas, images, meditations, vows, precepts, mantras, koans, stories and human examples. But each of these is a finger pointing to the moon. This "moon" (ultimate reality) is simply another way of experiencing our place in our world – not a peek at a distant heaven.

Over to You!

1. What foundational perspectives guide your thoughts and behaviour?
2. How do you handle the impermanence of living?
3. How would you define spirituality?

Contentment Here and Now

4.

Reflection: Ready for Adventure

The Shakyamuni Daibutsu Bronze[89]

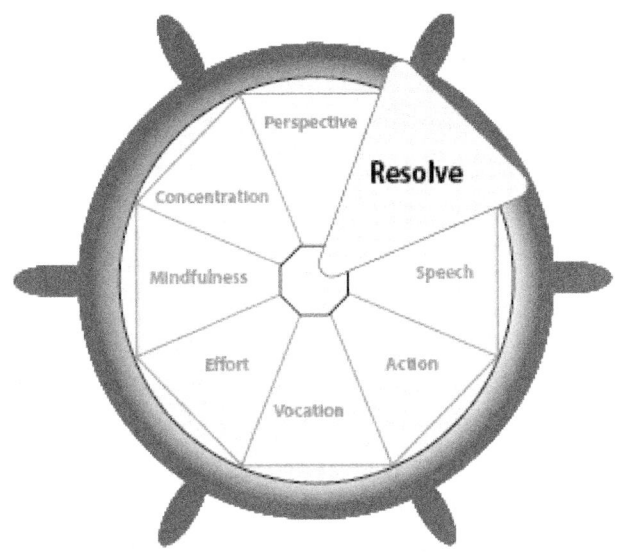

6.
Appropriate Resolve
(*samma sankappa*)

"Resolve means doing whatever it takes.
Resolve means reprioritising.
Resolve means change even if it's uncomfortable.
Resolve means saying no to something.
Resolve means saying yes to something else.
Resolve means this: This is happening and. I will make the rest of my life flow round it."
Louise Thompson[90]

"As you look back at the journey, you'll recognise how dedicated you were to achieving the goal and how deeply

you believed in yourself. You were fuelled by determination. And you may make the opposite observation when you don't reach an aim. You look back on the route to a goal you didn't complete and realise… your determination waned."
Elizabeth Perry[91]

"The Buddha has told us that while meditating prior to enlightenment, he found his thoughts could be divided into two opposite classes. Whenever he noticed thoughts of desire, ill-will, and harmfulness arising, he replaced them with thoughts of renunciation, goodwill, and harmlessness. He understood that the former thoughts lead to harm for oneself and others and obstruct the path to wisdom. Hence, he developed the wisdom to eliminate the obstruction and open the path."
David Dale Holmes[92]

Commitment is Essential

An appropriate perspective about ourselves and the world is crucial but insufficient. It requires 'resolve'. We need to commit ourselves to doing all that is necessary for Awakening. The original Pali word *sankappa* can mean intention, purpose, plan, and (more generally) thought.[93] We translate it as resolve because imitating Gotama's process of discovery includes his uncompromising commitment to find a resolution to his *dukkha*.

Gotama is pointing to something radically different from a strong dedication to self-centred purposes. His intention took him way beyond the securities, pleasures, and praises that motivate most of us. Outwardly, it was reflected in his commitment to serve others. Inwardly, it was driven by insights that cancelled the need for such ordinary satisfactions. Interestingly, Jesus, a spiritual adept who may well have encountered Buddhist thought and practice in his early years in Egypt (or perhaps India), argued that those who seek their own advantage will lose it – and vice versa – a thought with certain similarities to Gotama's.[94]

A Broader, Deeper Aim

The object of our resolve is as essential as its quality. Gotama is quoted as saying,

> "And what is appropriate resolve? It's a steadfast determination regarding renunciation, freedom from ill-will, and harmlessness."[95]

The aim of his resolve, broadly speaking, is to counter our narrow and sometimes brutal selfishness. This puts us on track for seeking our *enlightened* self-interest (pun intended), far from the narrow materialism and self-destructive pleasures that we might hope will answer our needs. Thus, the ultimate goal is not superficial and sensual forms of happiness (such as immediate gratification), but the deeper satisfactions of contentment.

Gautama provided two variations of his path. One was for monks and nuns; the other, for householders (laity). Both require the same resolve, but one is linked to many restraints and rules, while the other includes the pleasures and responsibilities of partnership, family life, and the wider community.

From Perspective to Resolve

The Buddha's formula of acknowledging and implementing the Four Ennobling Realities implies a progression from perspective to resolve. We begin with a desire to escape our personal dissatisfactions and are directed to helpful understandings that inform our search. 'Perspective' alone will not keep us progressing. Finding ultimate relief and escape from our *dukkha* requires both a clear goal and a determination to gain it. That is 'resolve'.

On an individual level, I came to see that I needed to adjust my habitual judgmentalism, and do the work required to shift away from this toxic reactivity. There was no once-for-all cure, Persistent correction was required, which required a strong resolve. Little by little my habit changed, as I reminded myself to shift from judging others (whose hearts and minds I could not know), to being mindful and corrective of my formerly unexamined self-righteousness.

More than Reason

We might expect that our emotions would be separate from rational thinking, but in Buddhism they are combined. My first Preceptor, Vairocana, has often expressed how Buddhist perspectives are simply the result of clear, intelligent thought. He says this in the context of understanding Gotama's concept of mind, which includes heart-felt feelings.

Reason and positive emotion can be seen as two aspects of the same thing. Rationality without kindness, compassion, empathy and equanimity is cold and inevitably misleading. But love without clear-sighted thinking is equally distorted.

Just as a bird can only fly with two wings, we need to join our vision of what is right with the desire to do so – and then persist with both. Perspective and resolve make a successful partnership.

Resolving to End Suffering!

One way or another everybody wants to end our dissatisfactions (*dukkha*). Suffering can ennoble us if it drives us to a resolve to do what is necessary for its elimination. The insight into the nature of our suffering, can dispose us to the third "reality" that our *dukkha* can end. From that point onward, we need the resolve to do what is necessary to end it (informed by the Eightfold Path).

But it doesn't end there. Ultimately, we will want to help alleviate the suffering of others, and ultimately all beings. Of course, at the beginning of our Buddhist journey this might be a distant goal or an unheard aspect of our dharmic yearning. But as we keep on the path, broadening our vision to more and more aspects of Gotama's teaching, the altruistic dimension will emerge.

Perhaps inevitably, we'll begin this journey without a full knowledge of its dynamic destination. We can mistake a milestone for ultimate goal. We might begin exploring Buddhism as a relief from our individual stresses and a contribution to our physical wellbeing. Or (as I did) we can identify with Gotama's movement as a confirmation of our existing values and experiences. These are not harmful intentions, nor inappropriate beginnings. But once achieved, they will not and cannot meet all our needs, and we will become hungry for new insights and practices… all the while moving closer to Awakening.

In her book on The Altruistic Urge, Dr. Stephanie D. Preston argues that our genetics contain a deep-seated urge to support the well-being of others. It begins with parental love for one's own children, but extends to the interests of tribal members, and ultimately to the human family.

We all can experience a desire for every being (including ourselves) to have a life free from avoidable suffering and to take some action for that to happen. Like love itself, universal altruistic urge is common in many spiritualities.

We Can Love Everyone

Traditional Buddhism (affirming innumerable rebirths) encourages us to increase our compassion for others by imagining that all beings were (at some time in our past lives) our loving mother. Regardless of our own experience, we can envision that all these mothers loved us unconditionally. It works for many, though far from everyone we be able to conjure up that feeling.

My preference is a practice that helps us cultivate universal kindness and compassion, based on the *Metta Sutta* (*the Discourse on Kindness*).

> "May all beings be at ease, happy and secure.
> Whatever living beings you may meet, weak or strong,
> With no exceptions:
> The influential and strong, the weak and insignificant,
> Whatever their stature medium, short or small,
> The well-known and the unknown,
> Those living near and far away,
> born and to be born.
> May all beings be at ease!"

This is meant to guide our attitude to others and ourselves twenty-four hours a day, seven days a week.

Practical Application

We are not urged to be so spiritually minded that we are no earthly good! Gotama saw how all actions begin in the mind. But he knew that thought alone will not get us anywhere. We can consider each of our own bright ideas in light of the questions, "Is it realistic?", "Is it helpful?", and "What is appropriate for my resolve?"

Of course, we alone, and even the actions of a group, cannot solve most of the problems that need addressing. But this doesn't have to hold us back. The "Star Thrower" fable by Loren Eisley[96] makes this point powerfully.

An old man walking on the beach encountered a child who was picking up starfish on the sand and throwing them back into the sea. "Why are you doing this?", he asked. The child replied, "The tide is going out. If I don't throw them back, they'll die." He chided her, "Don't you realise there are miles and miles of beach, with more starfish than you or I can save? You'll never be able to do it!" "Mister, you are right" he replied, then picked another up and returned it to the sea, adding, "It makes a difference for that one."

Middle Way thinking helps us avoid foolish excesses in our thoughts and actions – such as doing nothing or attempting too much – when some focused action might be helpful. We cannot 'save the world' but we can make a positive difference. Wisdom sometimes encourages us to pull back from actions that we cannot accomplish without harm to ourselves or others. In the face of all the needs in our global village, we need to determine what we can do and what action is not, at present, appropriate for us to attempt.

Besides compassion, we will benefit from a strong dose of humility. To "see ourselves as others see us" (Rabbie Burns) allows us to acknowledge both our imperfections and our strengths. This will keep us from wandering from the real world into fantasy land. Buddhist pragmatism is aware that our judgments, and those we've accepted from society, can be flawed. We are encouraged, therefore, to consider the opinions and attitudes of those we respect and do what seems to help.

Moving On from Self-Centeredness

My motivation was not like Gotama's "existential crisis". I had come to terms with sickness, suffering, and death. I was always hesitant to idealise "spiritual leaders", so I couldn't connect fully with the "fourth sighting" of a holy seeker. I thought I needed a community which was open to ideals that were important to me, such as non-violence. I wanted strong social reinforcement for my desire to escape the influence of materialism, power politics, and social or racial elitism. A lifelong learning junky, I was also seeking a group which excelled in teaching. In short, I was looking for a community that could re-live my youthful idealism.

I see now how these motivations were touched by a naïve, superficial self-centredness. They were also distorted by a judgmentalism that implied my motivations and understandings (if not my behaviours) were superior to others. Many of us begin that way.

Thankfully, impermanence, ineffability, and introspection have led me to shift my thoughts and intentions. I am more ready to recognise and heed *dharma* wisdom. It's a natural part of growing up (maturing). Perhaps most of us begin with a concern to relieve our own dissatisfactions and dilemmas.

When I began my Buddhist journey my intentions were not skilful, as defined by a more mature understanding. I'm sure this is a fairly common experience. But thankfully, once we get a taste of *dharma* values and insights, our motivations and consequent resolve can change.

Just as we cannot walk before we crawl, nor run before we walk, some of our needs must be satisfied before we have enough energy or motivation to go beyond them. Thus, the gradual or graduated reality of our *dharma* learning.

Progression is Gradual

Gotama's over-arching concern was to enable his audience to understand what was needed to improve their lives, and to challenge them to do it. He knew that all of us have our own sense of what we need. We will want to engage with what is appropriate to solving our pressing problems.

> "The Buddha didn't always teach mindfulness, the Four Noble Truths or *nibbana*. ... But [he taught] a Path, a way of consciously getting from 'where you feel you are' to 'somewhere better', whether that means just being able to give up smoking or drinking or being more at ease or less anxious that's always relevant to everyone." Ajahn Sucitto[97]

Tibetan Buddhists speak of a "graduated path" (*Lam-rim*), in which we learn to become a better person, step by step. That certainly has been my experience. As a 'learning junkie' I attended whatever classes were available in my *sangha*. My head knowledge increased almost on a daily basis. But my real dharma learning (applying the teachings in my life) only came when I was ready for them.

It would be a mistake to attempt developing every aspect of the Eightfold Path at once. Our graduated learning can best focus on just one thing at a time.

A Hierarchy of Needs and Satisfactions

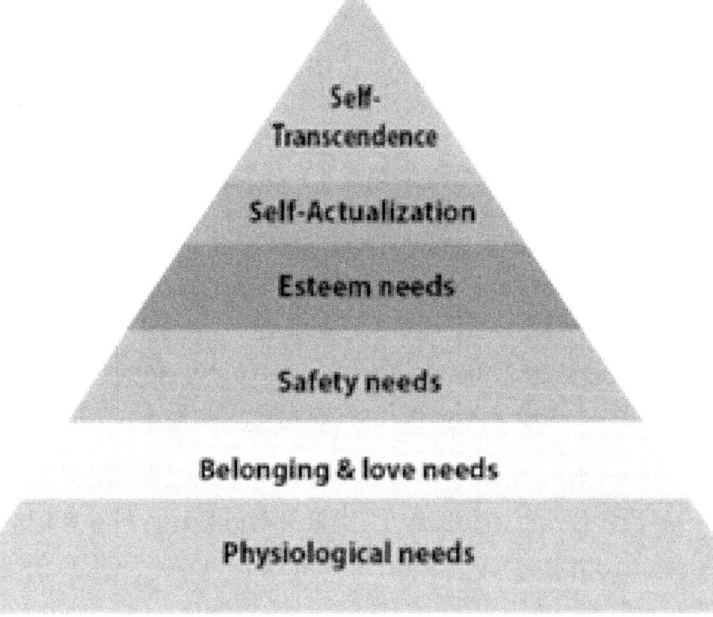

Abraham Maslow's Hierarchy of Needs

Psychologist Abraham Maslow has articulated a human needs profile that clarifies a developmental pattern from 'deficiency' to 'growth' to 'transcendence' – with each element building on the earlier stages. Thus, once satisfied, our food, clothing, and safety needs lead to our pursuing love and belonging, esteem, and self-actualisation.

This "theory of motivation" was published in 1943.[98] Decades later, Maslow came to recognise a 'higher' motivation beyond the limitations of self, relating to something greater. It is the "transcendence of the selfish Self".[99] We can understand the progress from survival needs to self-transcendence as a personal evolution. Buddhism encourages the same. Maslow sheds some new light on how the *dharma* strengthens and transforms us.

We can understand it in evolutionary terms: earlier iterations of our species were much more motivated by the demands of survival: food, security, reproduction, and the like. But 'the emergence of civilisation' promoted specialisations and consequent leisure time.

Religion developed for protection from uncontrollable forces and later an ethical sense that was increasingly altruistic. It included a developing sense of eternal Others (one or many) worthy of worship and requiring our attention. A parallel humanistic evolution explored spirituality without the need for God or gods. Gotama is part of this latter approach. Contentment is a companion and consequence of his highly evolved state.

Over to You!

Take five minutes or more of meditative quiet (perhaps with a consciousness of your breathing). Then draft a short, tentative (revisable) statement, consisting of the following:

1. What initial changes in your thinking might remove some *dukkha* from your life?

2. Using these insights, what actions are you taking to move towards a better life?

3. What opportunities do you have to remove the suffering of others?

Reflection: Companions

The Many Helping Hands of Kannon (Quan Yin)[100]

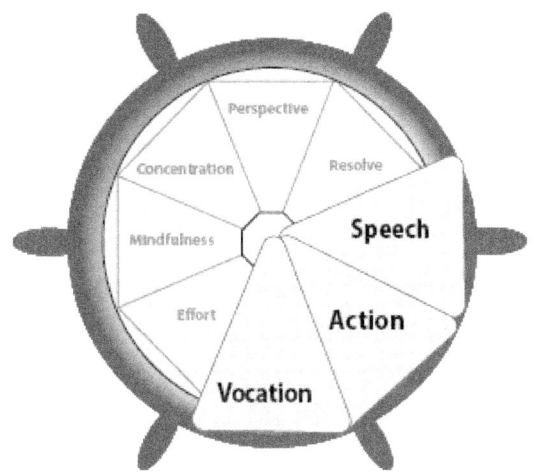

7.
Ethics: Appropriate Speech, Action, Vocation

"One man might conquer a thousand others in battle,
But the greatest of conquerors conquers himself."
Dhammapada, Verse 103 (author's paraphrase)

"**Ethical living is the indispensable condition of all that is worthwhile.**"
Ernest Caldecott, signatory of *The Humanist Manifesto* (1933)[101]

"**Ethical behaviour leads to and flows from an enlightened mind.**"
Seven Pillars Institute[102]

An Ethical Practice

Like Amos, Muhammad, and Jesus, Gotama stressed the importance of ethics for a healthy, holistic spirituality. The Buddha's guidance is not to meet the absolutist demands of an authoritarian figure. Rather, we are given the opportunity to help both ourselves and others move towards flourishing (*sukha*) and avoiding unnecessary suffering (*dukkha*) for everyone. Buddhist ethics, like every aspect of his *dharma,* are invitations rather than commands. We apply his teaching as we are ready – led by a sense of its relevance and our respect for those we admire and trust who exemplify its wholesome power.

Sometimes, like a tree in winter, our spiritual work is primarily internal, isolated from other people, and seemingly unrelated to the common good. But as surely as the spring and summer seasons, we are meant to leave our isolated shells and share the bounties of life with others – as many as possible. This outward work is essential for anyone on the Buddhist Path.

Gradually the *dharma* challenges us to be concerned beyond our individual concerns and needs. Crucially, but not unique to Buddhism, ethics takes us further than self-absorption. It provides a twin focus: ourselves and others.

Many believe we must be psychologically buoyant before we can reach out beyond ourselves. But I have found that a concern for other people brings a positive energy which can move us away from depression and anger. We might feel incapable of a robust ethical life, but by doing the right thing for others (and ourselves), even in small ways, we can become less obsessed with our perceived problems. The positive results and the enjoyment of helping others will encourage bolder and more consistent actions.

Gotama and his early interpreters never used the term "situation ethics", but it fits his thinking.[103] The prime intention is to be helpful to all beings; it needs to be applied with comprehensive mindfulness and creativity. John Dewey, the pragmatic philosopher, called this approach "reflective": "Reflective morality demands observation of particular situations, rather than fixed adherence to a priori principles."[104]

This approach implies that a rigid, rule-based approach to ethics will mislead us. Inflexible moral principles might seem to promise certainty and stability. This is ultimately impossible in a world marked by impermanence. Gotama's approach allows flexibility while not ignoring broad moral principles. The differences between his day and ours require us to consider how to make his views as relevant as possible to our present circumstances, which are so different from his. Yet his instruction is surprisingly relevant today. Human nature hasn't changed much in the past few thousand years!

Broad Principles, Not Rigid Rules

The Buddha did not promulgate a rigid ethical system to follow in all circumstances. Instead, he articulated broad principles and precepts for us to apply as they seem relevant to our specific situations.

The Dalai Lama, one of the world's most prominent advocates for the welfare of all sentient beings, exemplified a relaxed approach to ethics when he was recovering from a disabling condition. His physician advised him to abandon his vegetarian diet and to combat his illness with red meat. When he regained his strength, he returned to an all-veg diet.

Buddhist ethics require our discernment, sorting out many conflicting demands resulting from our needs and the needs of others. Even when the principles that motivate us are clear, we can keep learning how to apply them. For example, I am concerned how my life can most effectively respond to the climate crisis. I still drive a car, even though I anguish about how my life might respond to the climate crisis more effectively. This allows me to be more efficient and more helpful. But I keep adjusting my behaviour to be less harmful, for example, by walking and taking the bus more than ever before.

The Third Aspect: Appropriate Speech
(*samma vaca*)

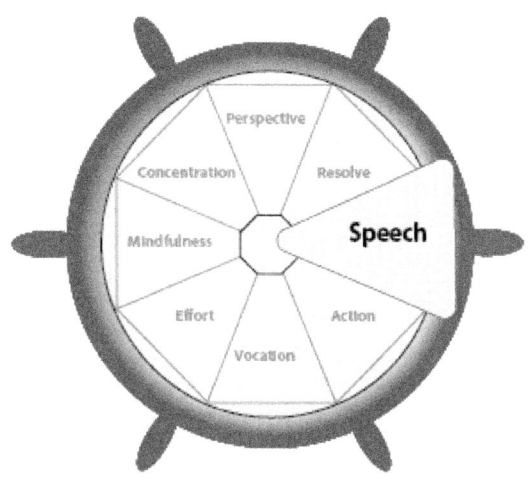

"The single biggest problem in communication is the illusion that it has taken place."
George Bernard Shaw[105]

Gotama stressed the importance of appropriate speech, the third aspect of his Eightfold Path. In Gotama's preliterate environment, voices were the primary means of exchanging our attitudes, perspectives, and information with others. His concept of what was appropriate is found in his Analysis of the Path (*Vibhanga Sutta*): "What is right speech? Abstaining from lying, abstaining from divisive speech, abstaining from harsh speech, abstaining from idle chatter: This is what I call right speech." These can be restated in positive terms: truthful, harmonious, gentle, and meaningful speech. The benefits are manifold and obvious. They can also be applied to more than our conversations with others, such as emails, texts, posts on social media, and publications of all sorts.

Truthfulness in communications is increasingly ignored today. Many (not all) politicians, advertisers, organisations, and individuals are willing to convey whatever will serve their interests, rather than relay all relevant information. A classic case is the tobacco industry's hiding the facts about smoking. But facts alone should not determine what we communicate. To be 'appropriate' or 'right' for Gotama was always in the context of what was beneficial to all those involved.

Ethics require an aspect of reflection. The present possibilities (and often social necessities) of instant responsiveness can get us all into trouble. Thankfully, some email programs allow us to retrieve emails right after sending them. The helpful cliché, 'Look before you leap!' applies to many aspects of modern living.

A simple formula conveys Appropriate Communication In the spirit of reflective ethics. Before approaching someone with a challenging message:

- Ask, 'Is it true?' If it's not, don't say it.
- If it is true, ask a further question: 'Is it helpful to others?' If not, don't say it.
- But if you consider it a constructive message, ask yourself, 'Is this the right time to communicate it?' If not, don't say it now, but decide on an appropriate time.
- If this is the right time, ask a final question: 'How shall I best communicate this?' Determine what is most helpful and least hurtful.

This four-fold approach may sound complicated and unwieldly. But if you realise the importance of each point, it can become natural and instinctual.

Nonviolent Communication is an approach advocated by many Buddhist leaders.[106] It was developed by Marchall B. Rosenberg, a trained psychologist who grew up in Detroit, Michigan. There he was confronted by violence daily. He called his new approach "a language of compassion". Rosenberg believed that conflict was inevitable, but violence is not. We all have needs, and we all are living in the same reality. If we discuss our differences in light of what we agree on, and with empathy for the other's needs, we can work to resolve our differences more easily than if we confronted them as adversaries.

The Fourth aspect: Appropriate Action (*samma kammanta*)

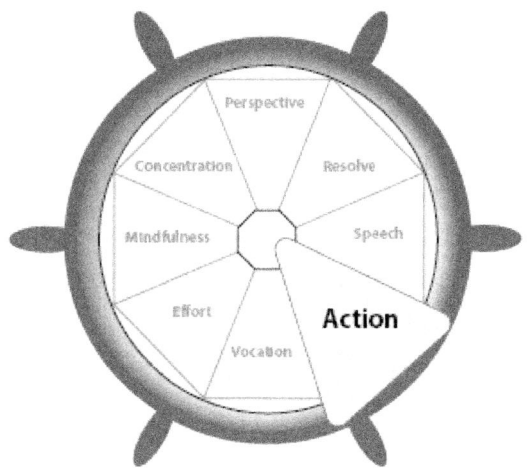

Gotama emphasises being aware of our minds (intentions, assumptions, and emotions) before we act. But he was aware of the need for actions to promote well-being and avoid harm, led by both wisdom and compassion. An unwise, inappropriate act can be well-meaning but counterproductive. Despite its emphasis on gaining inner peace not the "quietism" which many falsely associate with Gotama's advice. He promoted a Middle Way that avoided an obsession with results yet sought to make a real difference in the world. He knew that running away from problems and needs (our own and others) was neither enlightening nor effective. He mentioned to a follower named Sona (a former musician) that a stringed instrument needed to be tuned with the right tension – not too tight and not too loose. So it is with our talents, strengths, and energies. As a preacher once told me, 'If you are too heavenly-minded, you'll be no earthly good.' We dare not choose to sleep through the revolution if our goal is to awaken!

From early Buddhism onwards, monks and laity were urged to avoid intoxicating the mind, to refrain from killing other beings, to avoid taking what wasn't given to them, and to steer clear of inappropriate sex (such as intimate relationship with someone who is betrothed to another). The monks were expected to be chaste, lest their behaviour prove irresponsible and harmful to the villagers who provided them with their daily meal. Behind these injunctions is the certain knowledge that our minds are our most valuable asset and that the drive for physical satisfaction can lead us in directions that reason and compassion would have us avoid.

An interesting dialogue is recorded between Gotama and a silversmith named Cunda.[107] Their conversation began with the Braminic purification rites Cunda was following, but the Buddha quickly turned the discussion to the way we live our lives: 'Cunda, the purification rights of the brahmins are one thing, but my disciples focus on something else entirely. Their purification is to avoid unskilful actions.' He then told the silversmith that in his movement we strive to avoid dangerous mental, verbal and bodily actions. The "bodily actions" he thought harmful included, hunting and killing animals, taking what had not been given to them by the owners, and getting sexually involved with those who were not appropriate partners.

Much of Gotama's teaching is framed in the negative: avoiding harmful actions, rather than accentuating the positive behaviours we strive to achieve. Was this reflecting an ancient Indian mode of communication, or does it reflect a realistic appraisal of human nature? Perhaps the Buddha saw that if we refrain from doing harm, a natural tendency to be helpful and altruistic would lead us towards wholesomeness and contentment.

He knew the force of unhelpful thoughts and behaviours. Some were "fetters" which keep us from positive choices. Others were "hindrances" which blocked us from our natural wholesomeness. It is important to identify what nurtures the deepest possible contentment and incorporate it into our lives. But often it is necessary to realise what is holding us back and preventing the growth we long for – and take action to remove or neglect it. We do well to be guided by Gotama's advice that we should consciously determine what is helpful for our own well-being. It can include both the avoidance of what is toxic and embracing what helps us become the people we long to be.

The Fifth Aspect: Appropriate Vocation (*samma ajiva*)

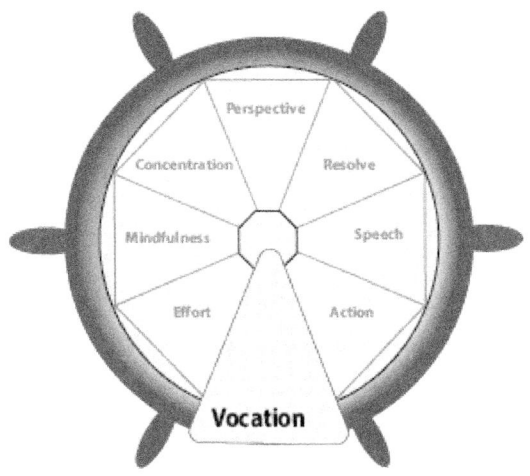

Gotama identified the need for some means of earning what is needed to support oneself and one's family. This, too, should be 'appropriate'. The monks and nuns required a minimum amount of food and possessions to support their very simple lifestyle. They earned their way by relying on the gifts of others, and returning a life of service, dedicated to the well-being of all. They modelled a life dedicated to Middle Way living, marked by compassion and kindness for all. This was their vocation.

His presentation of appropriate livelihood was focused more on the needs of householders. They were responsible for their family as well as themselves, and answerable to their Raj. We might equate this with contemporary needs to provide for one's immediate family and to pay our fair share of taxes to support the common good. Most of his followers would be part of the agricultural community: farmers with small holdings. Their labours would be contributing to the life and health of their families and their communities.

In Gotama's day commerce was developing, and non-agricultural professions were emerging. And there were some who supported the function of the autocratic states. Gotama chose to spotlight the livelihoods which were inappropriate for his followers, rather than list those that contributed to positive living. The Buddha spotlighted butchering, and the manufacture of poisons. Both would contradict the basic commitment to be helpful, not hurtful, to all beings. He did not, however, condemn policing and soldiering – both of which might be interpreted as restraining harmful behaviour.

Many people today avoid working for industries that are harmful to the public, to other beings, and to the balance of the natural world. But this is not always possible. Some converts to Buddhism in rural India were anguished because their only prospect of employment was in a munitions factory. If they quit, how would they provide for their families? The short-term solution was to keep working while they looked for a less destructive job, but also to realise the many positive opportunities to relate to workmates and management in a respectful and helpful way. We do well to avoid judgmental condemnation of those who are wrestling with such moral dilemmas. Their resolution can take a great deal of time. But when the opportunity is there, a vocation that benefits both self and others is appropriate.

Today we are conscious of the damage we continue to do to our environment and its dire consequences for the entire earth and its inhabitants. In our present Western context, would it also be useful to speak of 'appropriate consumption' as a key ethical concern?

A common misunderstanding is that we must have a particular 'calling' that is our eternal destiny. Some think that failure to discover our destined vocation is unacceptable. There might be some benefit in this view, but it is a mistake to think that we all need an unchanging sense of calling. A more dynamic understanding is to see that our appropriate vocation can change as we ourselves change and our circumstances keep shifting. If we concentrate on developing our character, we are more likely to apply our values and fulfil our responsibilities in whatever circumstance or activity we find ourselves.

Some Dangers on the Way

We can get stuck thinking that a vocation which seemed spot-on in the past is our never-ending calling. Similarly, we can feel our understanding of how to fulfil a particular value is right for all time. For example, I thought that when I embraced tithing (giving away a tenth of my income) that it should be the standard for everyone. Since then, I have modified my idea of giving. Monetary gifts are no longer primary. Giving of my time and engaging with other people (and animals) in helpful ways has taken pride of place in understanding "giving". I still share with those less fortunate who need the help of the charities I support. But when I do so, I factor in my needs and responsibilities and realise my time and expertise can be more important than my money. As well, I can see that generosity has no limits. Given the extreme needs of the world, limiting my giving to a tenth of my income might not be the appropriate figure.

As we consider "doing the right thing", we should be increasingly aware of the dangerous dynamic of simply fitting into other people's expectations. Many of us have, perhaps unconsciously, absorbed the standards of the crowd, our employers (or customers), and our parents. As we mature, we develop our own – and hopefully, find the courage to live by them when they conflict with others.

We should also be aware of the confirmation bias that leads us to identify Gotama's thoughts with our present understanding. I embraced Buddhism, for example, because it reflected my pacifist convictions.

Then, I adopted vegetarian and vegan practices, responding to my *sangha's* assumption that it represented Gotama's teaching. Now I realise that he never advocated either vegie or vegan as we understand the terms, although both are very positive life choices. My current dietary practice is not because of a specific directive from Gotama. Rather I am responding to his broad principle of no harm to sensory beings. When I affirm these practices, it is from solid ethical concerns and convictions, informed by realities such as the horrors of factory farming, the climate crisis, and the need to feed everyone on our crowded planet.

Similarly, we can find no explicit guidance regarding the present multi-crisis, including weapons of mass destruction, and the 'rules' that govern conflict. But the Buddha's broad ethical framework can inform our thinking on most ethical issues. This is the freedom of the *dharma* (and, at times, its burden). Expecting a simple "Buddha says so" will keep us disengaged from other issues that Gotama did not address.[108] Our conscience (the inner sense we develop of right and wrong) requires some fluidity considering our actions in their real-life contexts.

How we express and engage with any issue depends on our audience. What is appropriate in terms of my language might be very different when speaking to children, my neighbours, and my close friends.

Keep Moving Forward

We won't be perfect in every aspect of our ethical lives. But we can keep moving closer to the ideal. Our frustrations that we might have done better can be a powerful motivation for improvement. Changing circumstances and developing self-knowledge will reveal the need for further adjustments, even when our intentions are 'pure'. The best of us will know that we always can develop our ethical lives further.

Some meditations are like prayers (deep aspirations), in that they connect us with and strengthen wholesome desires. But we are not delegating the work of love to an omnipotent power. The best prayers, of whatever spiritual persuasion, are not, 'Do it for me', 'Solve my problem' or 'Resolve my dilemma', but rather 'How might I best respond to this opportunity?' In this sense, our meditation and other well-meaning thoughts will summon us to action from a heart-felt and well-considered position, to make a positive difference in other people's lives. We know we cannot do everything that's needed – yet we often can do something significant.

In its comprehensive sense, love engages our emotions and our will, demanding a measure of self-control. Whether our love leads to positive enhancements or suffering and destruction, depends on how we engage with the complexities of our intentions. Our physical and emotional needs can distort love's potential. Thus, Buddhist ethics includes training in sexual restraint, mindfulness, and moderation. Love in any of its forms avoids anything that would harm the object of our affection and attraction.

Over to You!

1. Can you identify a habit that would further develop your character?

2. How might you begin establishing it?

3. Do you need to adjust your work life or home life, to better align with the principles of appropriate speech, action, and vocation?

Reflection: Soaring

Meditating Buddha from a Rock-cut Stupa[109]

8.
Appropriate Effort
(*samma vayama*)

"In Buddhism, right effort is the practice of developing good qualities and avoiding unvirtuous thoughts and actions. The Buddha taught that some behaviours can help people achieve happiness, while others can prevent it."
Google AI Summary 15 August 2023

"Abandon whatever is unskilful, monks. If it were not possible to abandon the unskilful, I wouldn't tell you to do it. Nor would I say this if led to suffering. I am urging you to develop what is skilful because it benefits you and leads to pleasure."[110]
Kusala Sutta (Discourse on Skilfulness)

> "**Right effort puts us in gear. It sets our intention; we turn our energy in the best directions... Right Action is how we carry out that energy, intention, and determination—bringing wisdom and compassion to our actions.**"
> Judy Hagar, writing in *Quora*[111]

Mind-Training

It was clear to Gotama that we must understand our mind and know how to train it if we are to awaken. The final three aspects of Gotama's Path guide us to the crucial importance of Mind Training. No faith, philosophy, or self-improvement programme values the mind more than Buddhism. The opening verses of the Dhammapada underscore this:

> *"Mind precedes all states. They come from the mind. Mind is primary. Speak or act from an impure mind, and suffering follows like the wheel follows the ox as it draws the cart...*
>
> *"Speak or act from a pure mind, and happiness follows, like a shadow that stays with you."*

The three aspects of Mind Training are Appropriate **Effort**, Appropriate **Mindfulness**, and Appropriate **Concentration**. They are most often grouped under the banner of Meditation. Admittedly, meditation is a crucial Buddhist discipline, but Mind Training includes a much broader focus than that.

For monks, with their emphasis on meditative routines and with the limited scope of their other activities, this meditation can become an end in itself. As well as its immediate benefits (relaxation and insight) it provided "pleasant biding" for the monks. Thus, it was often perceived as the be-all and end-all of Buddhist "practice". Many Buddhist laity buy into this distorted thinking. But we must not limit our practice to meditation alone. The challenges arising from daily living requires a more comprehensive approach to Buddhist development through all aspects of the Eightfold Path and other parts of the Buddha's *dharma*.

Active, ethical living is crucially informed by our Effort, Mindfulness, and Concentration. These final three aspects of Gotama's Path, as the other five, need to be integrated into every part of our developing 'self' (body, mind, and emotions). Mind-training is about how we all might develop ourselves for a comprehensive practice involving our whole person. The mind is crucial. But mental practices such as meditation alone will not lead to full Awakening.

What Do We Mean by Mind?

What does 'mind' mean when Gotama uses the word? The primary term is *citta*, or 'heart-mind'. *Citta*'s response to events of every sort is both rational and emotional. Logical thinking is crucial. But so are the emotions which interpret and direct it. The two together are powerful forces for our Awakening and inner healing.

Citta is a great resource. It seeks both our own good with an enlightened self-interest and the good of others with an altruistic urge. Yet it also evaluates the practicality of our actions.

The power of the human mind to influence behaviour and to heal our bodies and emotions is becoming an accepted reality. When I first discussed my marriage difficulties with Toronto psychotherapist Dr Paul Vereshack, he told me early on, "Dennis, your mind is your greatest strength." I assumed it was a compliment on my brilliance. Now I see how he was trying to shake me out of my mental dullness – full of rationality but lacking a conscious connection with my emotions. He could see how little I was using my precious resource for healing my emotional life and gaining the strength to journey towards freedom. My *citta* needed to be trained!

The other words that Gotama uses for the mind can complement our understanding. *Manas* "often indicates the general thinking faculty."[112] It is a process that can operate independently of the five senses. It explores many dimensions of thought or experience and suggests appropriate responses. This aspect of the mind is oriented to action or decision.

A Comprehensive, Persistent Effort is Needed

If we develop Gotama's level of intentionality, all that we do and say will be shaped by our sense of what is in our best interests and the interests of others. A wise 'self-compassion' joined with a wise 'altruism' can keep us open to the needs of the moment. We need to 'make up our minds' to maintain a determination to be skilful at all times.

Informed by the dynamic realism of the *dharma*, we can choose what to reinforce and what to modify. We do ourselves a great deal of good when we examine our present pattern of thought and action, then improve it. This requires both confidence and courage – trusting the wisdom of *dharmic* analysis and responding appropriately to the challenges and opportunities of every situation.

How can we encourage ourselves to pursue and persist in appropriate efforts? We can reflect on and affirm all that we have learned and are learning each day. For many Buddhists (and non-Buddhists!) this includes a powerful morning routine to develop and strengthen our values, principles and purposes. Commonly our morning practice includes, at the very least, anticipation of the coming day, meditation, and expression of reasons to be grateful.

Our appropriate effort will draw upon each of the other seven aspects of the Buddhist Path. Ideally, it applies *dharmic* wisdom to the full range of our activities, always starting within our minds. But our efforts are not meant to end there. Insight is meant to lead to action.

Unnecessary Discouragement

Many have experienced the Awakening within their lifetime. We can take that journey to its intended end, if we recognise our true nature. We can greet unskilful thoughts and feelings with equanimity. Seeing them for what they are, we have the power to reject them, ignore them, and transform them. An example is Gotama experience of Mara's attacks while meditating. That devil meant to scare him off his quest. But the spears and arrows that were sent to harm him, were turned to flowers and fell short of their mark at his feet.

We can observe our thoughts and emotions for what they are but also understand how they can be altered if they are not conducive to our wholesome development. So many who seek Awakening fail to experience it simply because they gave up trying. Thus, a crucial virtue is unflagging determination (persistence). In fact, it is listed as one of the ten Buddhist perfections. And, of course, it is recognised in innumerable circles as a main virtue in many systems that guide us towards accomplishment.

Persistence

A Japanese proverb says, 'Fall seven times, stand up eight.' Many success gurus remind their audiences of Thomas Edison's persistence. Without it, we might all be relying on candles and lanterns at night. The story of the light bulb is one of continued determination. After he conceived of the basic concept, Edison tried 10,000 times to make one work before he succeeded. Patience, persistence and perspiration make an unbeatable combination for success, said Napoleon Hill, after studying the "secrets" of those who inspired him. He concluded that the majority lack it; but that it is a weakness that can be overcome by effort.[113]

Yet Gotama warned against excessive and stubborn persistence in a dialogue with Sona. He was a monk who was worn out and discouraged from his intense attitudes and emotions. Sona had been a musician, so the Buddha connected with that experience:

"Now what do you think, Sona. Before, when you were a house-dweller, were you skilled at playing the vina [a lute-like instrument]?" "I was indeed." "And when your vina had its strings too tight, could it play in tune?" "Surely not."

"And was it tuneful and playable when the strings were too loose?" "No, Master. It would sound terrible." "But when the strings were neither too tight nor too loose, could they then be tuned to the right pitch, Sona?" "Yes, indeed they could."

> "In the same way, Sona, too much persistence leads to restlessness, while excessively slack persistence leads to laziness. Thus, you should tune your persistence to what is your right pitch for you - not too slack, but not overly tight."[114]

As I grow older, I'm increasingly aware of the value of persistence. Looking back, I can see its power in the face of difficulties and obstacles. But I also recall many times when a lack of persistence kept me from fulfilling my responsibilities or gaining important outcomes. Now, having lost some of my youthful energy, I realise that I need to apply the principle of persistence more deliberately with many ordinary tasks that decades ago seemed simpler and took much less time.

The Illusion of Perfection

What are our efforts hoping to achieve? We are encouraged to avoid striving for a false and unachievable perfection. Although we wish to live without the disturbances of the three poisons (ignorance, greed, and hatred) it is impossible to completely escape their presence. The Buddha compassionately warned his followers that even a fully Awakened monk should expect his five senses to respond to life with both pain and pleasure.

Our humanity involves engaging with the world through our senses. This inevitably leads to subconscious reactions of attraction or aversion. These gut-level reactions occur in less than a second and can easily tempt us into poisonous reactivity. However, an Awakened consciousness recognises the poisons for what they are. At that point, we can respond skilfully, with *dharmic* wisdom and compassion before our reactivity leads to and ego-driven distortions and unwelcome actions.

For example, some Alcoholics may still sense a desire for a drink even after achieving sobriety. They do not have to give in to this desire and may well be encouraged that their resistance to self-harm strengthens with practice. At every stage of an Awakening life, we too may face strong temptations. When this occurs, we need to be aware of our latent reactivity and nip it in the bud.

Gotama spoke of disempowering the poisons of greed, hate, and delusion rather than eradicating them. He explained that their complete extinguishment only comes with death. In the discourse titled "The *Nibbana* [*nirvana*] Element", Gotama clarified that even when Awakened, we experience the natural tendencies of our five senses. Thankfully, in a state of *nirvana*, the three poisonous reactions are quieted. However, they may reappear from time to time, prompting a skilful response.

Fully realised disciples will not let these tendencies draw them away from equanimity. As he put it, if we are "stable and unattached," we will experience the "residue" of these reactions, but their power to distort wholesome living is gone. So when contemporary *arahants* (a Pali term meaning worthy or perfected) walk into their local shopping mall, they may see shiny new items and be attracted; but they won't feel compelled to buy them.

Four Crucial Efforts (*sammappadhana*)

"Restraint and abandonment,
development and protection:
these four strivings were taught
by the Kinsman of the Sun.
By these means an ardent *bhikkhu*
can attain the destruction of suffering."[115]

A major concept within Buddhism stemming from Gotama's teaching is the Four Efforts.[116] Appropriate Effort is linked to this four-fold analysis of our thoughts and behaviours. The purpose is to decrease our unskilfulness, which leads us into *dukkha* and skilfulness, leading us out of it. This broad framework needs to relate to our thoughts and actions – which can be both subtle and hidden. This analysis is pursued by conscious mindfulness and open, curious, listening meditation. It is presented in the form of self-interrogation.

The underlying question is, 'How can I be helpful to myself and others?' It takes us back to remembering the essential intention of the Buddhist life. This sixth aspect of the Path gives us a tool to help focus our thoughts and actions towards effecting our wisest intentions by asking ourselves four basic questions:

1. What is skilful and beneficial in my life? (These I should **strengthen and protect** from all that would erode or destroy them.)

2. What is toxic and unskilful in my life? (These I should **remove** as soon as I can.)

3. What positive qualities might **add** to my life? (I can benefit from cultivating any skilful insight and behaviour.)

4. What destructive qualities do I need to **avoid** and protect myself from their influence? (I need to be aware of their influence and to 'guard the gates of my senses'.)

Appropriate Effort thus includes cultivating what is beneficial to others and welcoming anything that will help us flourish. But we also need to recognise, remove, and reject whatever is harmful. These Four Efforts can be characterised as protecting and developing all that builds me up, plus uprooting and avoiding all that drags me down.

In the final quartile of my life, I am benefitting from applying such efforts in earlier years. They have added important qualities and patterns that I came to see were lacking in my life. Even now I am discovering ways to improve my vulnerable body (nutrition, exercise, sleep, and purposeful living). The older I get, the more time it requires – but it beats the alternative! Decades earlier, the effort was to heal my emotions – first through psychotherapy and then through various approaches, including *dharma* application. You will know what you need to welcome into your mind and behaviour. As with all self-development efforts, don't try to do everything simultaneously. 'Bite by bite' (or 'inch by inch'), we can gain significant change.

We might mention an important additional kind of effort (not unrelated to the traditional four): discernment.

Discernment is the ability to distinguish what is helpful and what is not. Two metaphors often used for this spiritual skill is 'separating the wheat from the chaff' and 'separating the gold nuggets from the silt' (derived from the gold rush days when individuals panned for precious nuggets in streams). We can also be vigilant in not being succoured into embracing the many scams and superficialities of our times.

Every insight and conviction needs converting to some action (mental and physical) to achieve its intended effect. In some situations, discernment requires courageous or sacrificial action, such as 'speaking truth to power' (at a political or personal level), abandoning a harmful situation we find ourselves in, or euthanizing a beloved pet when we discern that 'it's time'.

Personally, I've experienced a quantum leap in my ability to be useful when I realised that just articulating a thought (to myself) will not accomplish much. But when I thin k through its implications for action I can improve it immensely. Sometimes this discernment leads to a greater skilfulness in what I do and speak. But it often leads me to see that I cannot affect anything positive and need not invest my time and energy continuing with a mere imagination.

The Enemies of Awakening

A 5th Century CE Sri Lankan monk named Buddhaghosa wrote The Path to Purity (*Visuddhimagga*) [117], in which he introduced the concept of Near and Far Enemies of the *dharma*, which entrap us in unskilful living.

Near enemies are akin to 'Trojan horses', masquerading as benign companions. They are, in fact, imposters that lead us away from what is truly helpful.

A legend from the Trojan war is the tale of a defeat by mistakenly accepting a seemingly benign gift which was, in truth, a mortal danger. The Greek army pretended to retreat, leaving a large wooden horse sculpture as a peace offering. The city of Troy, celebrating their victory, was unprepared when, that evening, troops hidden inside the horse crept out and opened the gate for their compatriots to enter the city and slaughter their enemy. The moral of the story: Be vigilant always!

Near enemies are dangerously tainted with greed, hatred or delusion. These enemies may seem attractive, sensible, and compelling, but their real nature can be easily missed. They are often difficult to recognise for who they are because they can seem positive or harmless.[118]

The near enemy of kindness is sentimentality: an unhelpful emotional mode that can obscure what is really needed in a situation. Another near enemy of kindness is conditional love: warm wishes that easily evaporate when we see unwelcome qualities in the other person. The near enemies of compassion are pity and, again, conditional love.

Far enemies are more easily identified, but they can be difficult to avoid. Kindness' far enemy is ill will. Compassion's far enemy is cruelty. Could a Londoner in World War II feel kindness to the Nazi pilots and politicians who were dropping bombs on their city (43,000 civilians killed in eight months)? Could a victim of persecution or armed conflict feel compassion for their tormentor?

Can we rise above our relatively insignificant resentments and hurts? They may seem trivial in the greater sweep of history, but they can fill our hearts and minds and keep us from progressing on our journey to contentment.

We can extend this concept to any virtue. For instance, generosity's far enemy (the obvious one) is stinginess. It's near enemy (the subtle one) might be a sense of obligation or virtue signalling.

The Four Efforts paradigm warns us to guard the gates of our senses from destructive influences, and to expel them from our minds and hearts when we discern their presence. The near and far enemy distinction can be a great help in these tasks. For example, given the powerful forces inherent in our sexuality, we can be conscious of what we are seeking from each friendship – perhaps from every human encounter. The same self-consciousness applies to our relationship to money, influence, and power. Over time, we can gain a penetrating understanding of ourselves, including our habitual behaviours and the mindsets behind them. If we are not consciously asking, 'What is appropriate for me in this situation?' we might ignore the dangers of our many near and far enemies.

The situations we face might not lend themselves to simple formulae. But concepts like the Four Efforts and Near and Far Enemies can provide a practical framework for engaging with all the influences and invitations before us.

Effort Isn't Everything

There are no guarantees of consequent achievement simply because we are trying harder. Some of the current discussions on manifesting (achieving our determinations) imply that if we choose an outcome and act consistently to realise it, it will happen.

It is good to keep in mind that we cannot control the future by our efforts. In an opportune situation, what we do will achieve our aims. Circumstance sometimes intervenes. Some are headwinds (slowing us down) and some are tailwinds (speeding us forward).

My father, a self-made man and workaholic, always delighted telling a story about a well-known industrialist of an earlier era. The industrialist was asked, "How did you become so wealthy?". His response. "My family were impoverished by the Great Depression, so we had no resources. One day, a friend gave me an apple. Even though I was hungry I had the sense not to eat it but to sell it on the street. The proceeds were enough money to buy two apples, and I was disciplined enough to keep multiplying my stock until I had a tidy business as a street vendor. Then a distant uncle died and left me 200,000 dollars!" Similarly, we can be blessed (or cursed) by circumstances not of our own making.

If our efforts are undercut or reversed by factors beyond our control, perseverance and equanimity are two virtues that can help us move forward against the tide of adverse forces and unforeseen complications.

Authenticity is Required

Our chosen outcomes and our efforts are most effective and satisfying when they are deeply authentic. Equanimity comes most easily to a mind and heart that is in harmony with itself, as do all the virtues. Without that we will not be perceived by others or ourselves as truthful, reliable, and trustworthy individuals. If we find ourselves conflicted and hesitant about meeting the expectations we put upon ourselves, including those we accept from others, it will undermine our confidence and self-belief – and sometimes weaken others' confidence in us.

With authenticity we will not only feel better about ourselves we are more likely to attract the interest and cooperation of those with whom we want to associate.

I've experienced 'inauthentic' self-imposed aspirations, but also its opposite. One is full of anguish, the other full of joy. But the *dharma* has convinced me that I can only know who I am now (not for all time). Looking ahead, I can only be sure of what I want to become as I continue to develop. I might be clear about my learning goals and my achievement-oriented objectives. But none of us can really know what lies ahead. Thankfully, Gotama has given us a developmental programme that is equally helpful in good times and in not so good times.

Open to the Unexpected

Secular Buddhism can seem to reflect hubristic confidence in our ability to know everything worth knowing and to do all that can be done. By linking realism to science (treated as an established consensus about 'reality') we can easily dismiss anything that is not 'scientifically' validated. Yet there is extensive evidence that our conception of reality has been unexpectedly reversed time and time again. This is the arrogance of 'scientism'. Humanism (an unswerving focus on human values and human capabilities) can make the same miscalculation.

We can easily mistake our ability to affect our environment as the only force outside of nature's own energies that can do so. Yet we may well be missing something: What if some of the "tales of the supernatural" and "intimations of immortality" (beyond our present fallible knowledge of the natural world) might have something to them. Of course, we'll never know for sure.

Despite the lack of a scientific explanation, synchronicity is a common experience: circumstances which have no apparent causal connection conspire to impact our lives for the better (and sometimes for the worse). We can simply note the effects as chance or leave them open to unverifiable, uncertain conclusions. The unexpected and unmerited good that comes our way may be easily attributed to a theistic or *karmic* source, but we cannot be sure of any explanation.

In Randall Jarrell's ironic poem, *Hope* we are advised that while it seems we know all the cards that have been dealt us – thus defining our expectations of life – we don't and cannot have a certain knowledge of what the day will bring.

> In Folly's mailbox
> Still laughs the postcard, Hope:
> Your uncle in Australia
> Has died and you are Pope,
> For many a soul has entertained

> A mailman unawares --
> And as you cry, Impossible,
> A step is on the stairs.

Whatever lies in our 'mailbox' (and whether we open it with hope or dread) it is helpful to try to be discerning about the events and energies that come our way, even if we cannot understand them with a convincing clarity.

Over to You!

1. When have you demonstrated persistent efforts that have resulted in beneficial outcomes?

2. Are there any areas of your life that deserve your persistent efforts?

3. Are you living authentically? If not, how might you adjust?

CONTENTMENT HERE AND NOW

4.

Reflection: Fed by a Friend

Contentment Here and Now

Spring Buddha[119]

9.
Appropriate Mindfulness
(samma sati)

"Try to be mindful, and let things take their natural course. Then your mind will become still in any surroundings, like a clear forest pool. All kinds of wonderful, rare animals will come to drink at the pool, and you will clearly see the nature of all things."
Ajahn Chah[120]

"By observing our experiences and allowing them to be as they are, we can cultivate a sense of contentment and gain freedom from habitual thought patterns. This can help to release us from loops of stress, depression and anxiety."
The Mindfulness Project[121]

"When we practice right concentration, we're practising bringing the mind in harmony with the other aspects of the noble Eightfold Path."
Bradley Donaldson[122]

"What do you think about this?" said the Buddha. "What is the purpose of a mirror?" "It is for the purpose of reflection, sir", replied Rahula. "Even so, an action to be done by body, speech or mind should only be done after careful reflection."
Ambalatthikarahulovada Sutta[123]

What Mindfulness Can Bring to Our Lives

Mindfulness is crucial for our development. Gotama's Awakening came from a vivid realisation of how to best understand himself (his 'self') and his true advantage in a fresh way. Mindfulness of human nature led to his most penetrating insights. He developed a conviction of the necessity of mindfulness for constructive living. The more we apply mindfulness to our self-awareness, the more it supports our Awakening.

What is mindfulness? The Pali word *sati* can be translated as memory (recall), but it is more frequently rendered as 'awareness' and 'mindfulness'.

In India, meditation and mindfulness were a preoccupation for some thoughtful individuals prior to Gotama's time. But it grew immensely through the movement he established. Mindfulness has been an emphasis in other contexts. Ancient Greece and Rome had parallel interests. Today it is a hot topic for business leaders, athletes, health professionals, and the wider public.

Neuroscience continues to add many new dimensions to our understanding of this approach.

> "Research over the past two decades broadly supports the claim that mindfulness meditation — practiced widely for the reduction of stress and promotion of health — exerts beneficial effects on physical and mental health, and cognitive performance. Recent neuroimaging studies have begun to uncover the brain areas and networks that mediate these positive effects."[124]

It would be unhelpful to think that Gotama's views yield the final word on this subject. But he does provide a framework for us to develop this crucial component for both our spiritual growth and our mundane functioning.

The Modern Mindfulness Movement

Thanks to the contemporary Mindfulness Movement, some aspects of Gotama's original concept have entered Western consciousness. Search for articles, apps, courses, and organisations devoted to facilitating mindfulness, and you'll find near-inexhaustible resources.

Mindfulness is an essential part of many programmes for stress relief, healing, self-development, worldly success and spiritual mastery. We find this within many disciplines, including medicine, psychology, neurology, self-development, and spirituality.

Mindfulness has become a popular concept through a movement initiated and guided by Dr. Jon Kabat-Zinn. Thanks to his tireless work, courses in Mindfulness-Based Stress Reduction and Mindfulness-Based Cognitive Therapy are widely available. They have touched many millions of lives and sparked a movement that is bringing accredited mindfulness teaching, coaching, and counselling to hundreds of thousands of those who seek stress relief and self-knowledge.

Kabat-Zinn has summarised mindfulness as "Paying attention on purpose, in the present moment, and nonjudgmentally." When applied regularly, these three qualities reduce stress and provide a measure of freedom from habitual or impulsive responses.

Jon Kabat-Zinn[125]

"When we can actually be where we are, not trying to find another state of mind, we discover deep internal resources we can make use of. Coming to terms with things as they are is my definition of healing." Jon Kabat-Zinn (*Shambhala Magazine*)

Meditation is the key training for the modern approach to mindfulness. It is not unrelated to Buddhism because Dr. Kabat-Zinn learned it while attending Zen gatherings.

Nine Positive Insights

An organisation that calls itself The Mindfulness Project, has listed nine "Common Misconceptions of Mindfulness".[126] This prompts me to list of nine positive insights about a secular approach to mindfulness meditation:

1. Mindfulness puts us in touch with the many thoughts and emotions that constantly register in our minds. This contributes to our self-understanding.

2. A regular mindfulness practice (such as meditation) allows all our busy mental traffic to pass on, saving us from holding onto passing thoughts A common image is that each thought can be like a cloud in the sky – appearing and then moving on. This encourages us to see that we need not be prisoners of our thoughts and feelings. When they present themselves, we can let them go.

3. By focusing on a concentration point (such as our breathing or a sunset) we can shift our attention from transient mental events.

4. Mindfulness is cultivated both formally (through meditation) and informally (by applying it in our daily activities). In a sense, the purpose of a conscious period of mindful "practice" is to develop our ability to be constantly mindful.

5. Meditation can be an effective method for achieving the goal of mindfulness. But it yields many other benefits, clustering around relaxation and insight.

6. Mindfulness takes us beyond specific objectives. It will exceed your specific expectations if you hold

your thoughts lightly. An intention to be mindful throughout our waking hours will enhance our lives.

7. Mindfulness can be practised 'anytime, anywhere, by anyone'.

8. Mindfulness Meditation is not wholly predictable. Expect some delightful surprises. Some experiences will seem more satisfactory than others. But a regular practice to develop sati will prove effective.

9. Finally, meditation is not the only way to develop and maintain mindfulness. Any means of perceiving the realities within and outside our individual existence is useful and worth cultivating. This can include journalling, listening to 'soul music', reflecting on poetry or prose, and exposure to nature.

Buddhist Mindfulness

Many people think of mindfulness as awareness of what is happening or exists in the present moment. Developing our awareness in this way allows us to recognise more of the input our senses gather. This, in turn, permits us to consider the significance and consequence of what is registering in our minds and bodies.

Gotama alerts us to strive for something more than simply living in the moment (the 'now'). *Sati*, the original term that Gotama chose to use, has a root meaning of 'memory' (recalling). It is more than a consciousness of our surroundings and our response to it.

What is it that we are supposed to remember? First and foremost, it is the *dharma*, especially the Four Realities and the Eightfold Path. A mindfulness of impermanence puts everything into perspective. A mindfulness of the nature of our dissatisfactions is a great asset. Greater still is remembering how Gotama said we need not be stuck with them. Buddhist Mindfulness also includes a realisation that we can look beyond our present frustrations. We can transcend our experience and apply the teachings that make our moments hopeful and positive for us and for others. It is easy to forget the *dharma* in the midst of our disappointments and dissatisfactions (our traumas and tragedies) But when we bring the teaching into our consciousness, it is like a healing ointment applied to a wound.

Transformation

Mindfulness is meant to be transformative in a radical way. It contributes to an awareness of our environment and inner processing of it. But, as we remember to include *dharmic* perspectives we become aware of our flexible natures, which leads to living with freedom and joy.

> "Buddhism is a way of life based on the training of the mind. Its one ultimate aim is to show the way to complete liberation… Its immediate aim is to strike at the roots of suffering in everyday life." Leonard Bullen[127]

This understanding of mindfulness counters the mistaken apprehension that it is "all about" escaping from the pressures of life through meditative retreat.

The first chapter in Rick Hanson's *Neurodharma* (2020) argues that science has recently revealed that we can strengthen and modify our neural pathways to our advantage.[128] Mindfulness, he asserts, doesn't eliminate our ego function (our sense of self and our ability to choose and act). But it does transform it. Hanson argues that releasing our consciousness from the limitations of rigid egos is the ultimate gift of the *dharma*, registered in our moment-by-moment awareness. *Sati*, from a Buddhist perspective, provides a fresh view of the universe and of ourselves within it.

A Developmental Journey

In the early stages of our *dharma* development, Buddhist mindfulness might seem unnatural and cumbersome – either irrelevant to our present understanding of ourselves or frightening in the implied demands. But an intentional mindfulness practice, when it becomes a natural part of us, will move us towards an effortless spontaneity and satisfaction.

An example from my early days as a Buddhist (when my knowledge of the teaching was quite limited): I walk past a shop selling the latest gizmo. Instinctively (led by my reactive conditioning), I want it and work out a quick plan to get it. Then I consider, "This is grasping after something that might be thrilling for a while, but it's a time waster; buying it will leave me with less money to save for what's more important." Other experiences may be more subtle and complicated, but the complex simplicity of the *dharma*, as we practise it, yields its wisdom clearly – appropriate to our situation and understanding at that time.

Mindfulness is a key to achieving a progressive deepening of consciousness. It takes us from conscious awareness of sensory input towards a sense of peace and personal integration and ultimately to sensing our union with the universe, "no-thingness". These states of consciousness are known as the *jhanas*. As we move towards this unusual experience, our ego-sense can be permanently softened.

Mindfulness can relate us to the many factors both within and without our individual 'selves'. This helps us connect with the external world in a more helpful way. An example from a recent conversation I had about the Israel-Palestine conflict. My friend and I had quite different opinions and underlying assumptions. We both felt strong emotions about this tragic subject. To the extent that we could be mindful of our own reactivity and rigidity of thought, we had a chance to talk as two concerned human beings coming from very different positions. A mindfulness of the values and skills relevant to a conversation like this could direct us to a greater openness and fuller listening to the other. And it happened! It wasn't perfect, but it was substantially better than a go-nowhere argument. Instead of harsh replies to her assertions, I could ask for clarification. Later, I can think through an approach that might help me sharpen or revise my own "position".

A Personal Example

During a walk, I can find myself unnecessarily lost in my thoughts and miss the scene around me. Whether I am using the walk to explore an important thought or simply random daydreaming, I am losing touch with the present moment. When I do realise that and recall the benefits of a broader mindfulness, I open myself to the many streams of experience it presents: the wind on my face, the shapes of the trees (each different and each containing many different aspects of the life force), the sensation of hot and cold, the curve of the path, the sensations that come with each step, my emotions and fleeting thoughts, and the enthusiasm of my canine companion. As I pass other walkers, I notice the expressions on their faces and often respond to each with a smile and an apt phrase.

By getting out of my head and experiencing my senses more directly, I become aware of the multifaceted beauty around me and the complex responsiveness within me. Whether out walking or in any other context, mindfulness makes me more aware of my own reactivity and thus enabled to shift it to something more helpful.

Mindfulness can be one of the most powerful means of moving us towards Awakening. The popular understanding of its nature and use can be expanded by learning how Gotama understood awareness. Once we have learned to apply mindfulness in our lives and relate it to the other seven aspects of the Eightfold Path, it can be our primary dynamic for growth.

Over to You!

4. What characteristics of mindfulness are most familiar to you?

5. What are the effects of your mindfulness or meditation practice?

6. What do you want to explore further about mindfulness?

A SECULAR BUDDHIST SPIRITUALITY

Reflection: A Mysterious Beauty

An Awakened Celt[129]

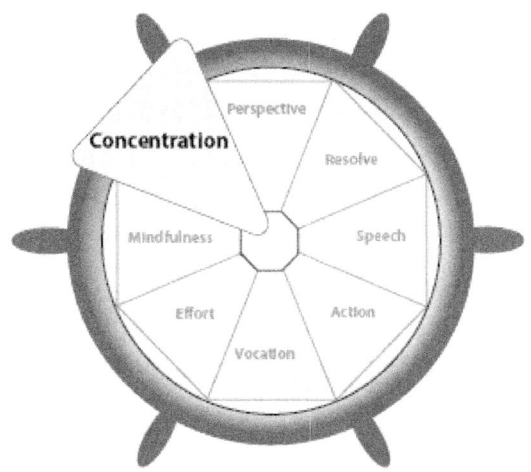

10.
Appropriate Concentration
(*samma samadhi*)

"When every physical and mental resource is focused, one's power to solve a problem multiplies tremendously."
Norman Vincent Peale

"Concentrate all your thoughts upon the work at hand. The sun's rays do not burn until brought to a focus."
Alexander Graham Bell

"When walking, walk. When eating, eat."
Zen Proverb

A Special Kind of Consciousness

Concentration is the final aspect of the path to Awakening. *Samadhi's* root meaning is "to place together". The term refers to the state in which the subject and the object (conceived as self and other) merge into one. When our consciousness is integrated with a particular experience, in that moment it is fully concentrated. It's a moment of self-forgetting, often described as absorption. This can refer to unswerving attention in meditation or concentration in any other experience. It may be very brief or quite prolonged. In *samadhi*, you will have a sense of presence with little 'me' in it. It's not a conscious mutuality (me with the other), but a moment in which 'being' and 'doing' are one.

When writing, I sometimes simply enter the process with little sense of anything other than being in the moment at hand. I forget ordinary concerns and do what I am doing with an all-consuming focus. I forget when it's time to eat, having lost my normal mealtime hunger. Concentration can increase the quality as well as the quantity of my output. Like me, some people wait to begin a project until they are relatively close to the deadline because they're counting on the power of concentration to work its 'magic'. Of course it always won't work out that way!

Likewise, when I'm present in a concentrated way with a natural 'object', whether a starry sky, stormy sea, ancient tree, or young child, the benefit of these moments is immeasurably more than when I give them less than my full attention.

In meditation, if we become absorbed in an object, perhaps focusing on our breath or repeating a mantra, our consciousness can change. No longer do we need to encourage distractions to pass from us; we simply are not distracted. When our concentration deepens, we become increasingly absorbed in a sense of unified presence. It is described as an awareness of nothing (no separate thing) and everything (an awareness of the greater whole), into which we are indistinct as a separate presence. The normal sense of calm and refreshment is increased greatly.

When our meditation focus is seduced by a multitude of objects, emotions, thoughts, and responsibilities, we lose the concentration emphasis. With training, we all can experience the benefits of an extended focus. Thich Nhat Hanh was insistent that we should avoid unnecessary distractions His approach was to, 'Concentrate on what you are doing. When you are meditating, just meditate. When you are washing the dishes or sweeping the floor, don't chat with anyone; focus on the task at hand.'

In such experiences, time seems to freeze or disappear. I have experienced a normal half-hour meditation extended to three hours without any sense of its prolonging. But thirty minutes can seem interminable when I am not concentrating and perpetually wondering if the allotted time is up. As we learn from meditation, every concentration point is an escape from time's inexorable progression and an entrance into a different orientation, with a wonderful refreshment resulting.

When we concentrate, we experience a sense of stability, a dynamic permanence. On reflection, we may admit that everything we perceive is indeed impermanent. But times of escaping this awareness by being in the moment alters our mental and bodily processing of it.

Flow

A contemporary concept, vitally related to concentration is that of "Flow". Mihaly Csikszentmihalyi (pronounced 'me-high-chick-sent-me-high') is noted for his decades of work developing the concept of Flow, which he describes in his book on *The Psychology of Optimal Experience*.[130] As he understands it Flow has eight characteristics in a person's experience:

1. Our actions and awareness are merged by concentrating on a task or activity.
2. We have clear goals and rewards for our work and thus can know when we are succeeding.
3. Our sense of time is transformed. Some say it speeds up; others think it slows down.
4. Our experience is intrinsically rewarding.
5. Our activity seems effortless.
6. We sense a balance between challenge and skills.
7. We lose the need to verbalise what they are doing.
8. We feel in control of the task.

Undergirding Csikszentmihalyi's study of flow was a concern for happiness.[131] Seeing the psychological devastation of the Second World War, he wondered, "What makes life worth living? What brings us happiness?" Finding and sharing the answers (of which flow was a crucial component) became his life mission. The way to a contented life, he came to see, does not lie outside us but within. This was not a unique insight. The Taoist concept of *Wu Wei* ("effortless effort") is a flow state in which we become part of the action we're involved in. Aristotle's concept of *eudaimonia* (flourishing) relates well to Csikszentmihalyi's understanding. And it rings true to Gotama's emphasis on concentration.

Flow, and thus concentration, is one of the ongoing discoveries of neuroscience. In 2021 a research team reported on some of the current understanding of the Flow State, from a neurological perspective. This research confirmed that in Flow our frontal lobes may regulate behaviour automatically, not through conscious effort. "The prefrontal areas of the brain were quite active during flow. However frontal areas relating to self-reflective thinking were less active."[132] When we have self-referential thoughts, such as worrying or boasting, our concentration is low. When we are focused away from ourselves, with a challenging yet doable task, thought, or perception, our attention keeps flowing. If the task is too easy, our minds wander. This concurs with meditative concentration and absorption, in which our sense of personal presence is faint but not altogether absent.

Levels of Consciousness

Contemporary psychology and neurology have revealed many crucial insights about our minds. No matter how much we analyse it, there remains a good deal of mystery about the ultimate source of our thoughts and feelings. Yet we have many helpful insights not available to Gotama. I am impressed that many of his thoughts are not contradicted by our science.

At present, there is no consensus about the nature of consciousness and the forms or levels in which it exists. My current understanding is as follows.

Our **conscious** awareness experiences life through the six senses, including our thoughts. We observe and categorise these events, with the power to analyse, compare, and make decisions. When we consider the *dharma*, define a flourishing and contented life, develop action plans to achieve our chosen goals, and evaluate our actions and thoughts we are using our conscious minds. We are conscious of ourselves (self-consciousness).

Our **subconscious** operates below the radar of our thoughts and our self-consciousness. It provides automatic reactions, to keep us safe and aid our survival. But it also is a storehouse of learned activities. It relates to the phenomenon of "muscle memory". For example, the subconscious allows concert pianists to play the 108 keys on the Beleura Grand Piano from a memorised score. At a more common level, the subconscious allows many of us to ride a tricycle, and drive a car automatically, without having to think about it.

Our **unconscious** mind regulates our behaviour with an assumed sense of what is appropriate and what is not. These unconscious functions are learned – some through conscious effort and others by a kind of social osmosis (from parents, peers, the wider social consensus, and the influence of advertising, etc.). Genetically determined personality traits can be included here as well. The subconscious contains our memory bank, sometimes with its own versions of what happened and what it meant. It shapes our moral impulses (conscience) and our emotions. Traumatic events can be "hidden" in the unconscious mind yet generate much that is observed by others or intrudes into our conscious thoughts.

A possible fourth is our **supra-personal consciousness**, which helps to explain some other experiences: those dimensions of our 'selves' that cannot be supported by internal influences. It seems to come above and beyond all identifiable sources. As such it can feel mysterious, beyond scientific calculation. But its reality is felt. Something is there.

An Integrated Consciousness

When all levels of our consciousness are integrated, with no conflicting perceptions, our concentration is natural and spontaneous. This increases the quality and effect of our efforts immeasurably. It enhances our sense of well-being and our ability to connect with others, as they sense our authenticity. This integration leads to the deepest level of satisfaction. As the final aspect of the Eightfold Path, it can be considered to contain the other seven. As such, it gives us a crucial insight into Awakening - Gotama's and our own.

Over to You!

1. What are your experiences of concentrated thinking (in meditation, perceiving nature, or in the midst of some task)?
2. How might you cultivate more concentration in your life?
3. How much has your consciousness (your perceptions) created the person you are now?

CONTENTMENT HERE AND NOW

A SECULAR BUDDHIST SPIRITUALITY

Reflection: Full Moonlight

Meditating Buddha[133]

11.
Effective Meditation

"Feelings come and go like clouds in a windy sky. Conscious breathing is my anchor."
Thich Nhat Hanh

"Just as with her life mother will shield her only child from hurt, let all-embracing thoughts for all beings be yours."
Metta Sutta

"A little bit of *om* can make a big bit of difference. The world is split into two groups: those that already get meditation and those that don't. For some, it is quite literally the greatest thing they've ever done. For others, it's just sitting on the floor wondering when 'it' is going to happen."
Trekstock Website (for young adults living with cancer)[134]

A Meditation Catechism

Meditation is a quintessential part of Buddhist practice. The following catechism, in question-and-answer format, provides an understanding of some of the core practices and beliefs surrounding meditation.

What is meditation?
Meditation is a practice in which we concentrate on a single object or the constant flow of sensory input, to calm our minds and emotions, and experience beneficial insights.

Why should I meditate?
We meditate to calm our restless minds, relax our bodies, and gain the insights that lead to full Awakening.

How many meditations are there?
There are numerous meditations. Some are described in the earliest discourses. Some were developed after Gotama to suit the expectations and preferences of different traditions and cultures (Indian, Chinese/Japanese, Tibetan, Western, and many others) and the preferences of individual personalities.

We can meditate sitting, walking, and lying down. Our meditation can emphasise relaxing and destressing (*samatha*) or insight (*vipassana*) – but all meditations potentially contain both elements. Meditation can be based on sight (actual and imagined), sounds (including mantras and bellringing), our bodily sensations, our thoughts, or an open-ended mindfulness of all sense input (Chan and Zen). As per the Asian saying, "There are 84,000 ways to meditate".

Do the different meditations have anything in common?
Most have a concentration point or a theme upon which they direct their attention. Most are relaxing and insightful.

What if you're distracted, or your mind wanders from the concentration point?
It happens to all meditators. For the most beneficial meditation, once you know that your attention has

wandered, you return to the concentration point. Avoid judging yourself negatively. Rather than blame yourself, praise yourself for reestablishing your concentration.

Is Buddhist Meditation the same as Mindfulness Meditation?
The modern mindfulness movement stresses a nonjudgmental awareness of the present moment, which relieves stress (*samatha*). Buddhist Meditation can do the same, but it includes insight into your mind and behaviour (*vipassana*). The emphases of the meditation teacher and the engagement of the meditator determine which features are included.

How can we calm ourselves and destress through meditation?
By concentrating on something particular (for example, our breath, the sound of a bell, the cultivation of kindness, the sensations of our bodies, a candle flame), we remove the labour and stress of shifting our attention from one thing to another. This is both relaxing and rejuvenating. These are *samatha* practices.

How do we gain insight through meditation?
By considering Impermanence as a universal phenomenon, including our Impermanence, examining the nature and origin of our responses to our thoughts and experiences, and reflecting on Gotama's teachings and example.

Must we meditate to awaken?
Meditation develops mindfulness and helps you confront and overcome the barriers to Awakening. When linked to the ennobling Eightfold Path, it is a proven aid to gaining and sustaining contentment. Regular meditation is vital for your continuing vitality unless you know a better way.

Tame the Monkey

Gotama spoke of "monkey mind". As a monkey in the forest will grasp a branch, then release it to leap to the next, then to others, our conscious minds keep jumping from one thing to another.[135] Over time, meditation will reveal our monkey minds. What motivates the monkey? He's bored and hungry for meaningful moments; he has the restless energy of a toddler. As we pursue Awakening by walking the Eightfold Path and meditating regularly, we counter boredom with a purposeful effort that results in more profound satisfactions than the superficial monkey movements can gain. As we settle into our habitual meditation position, we set our intention to exchange the frenetic pace of our lives and the constant bombardment of our senses by commercially driven media for a time-tested neurological refreshment. The trapped tensions within our bodies are released. We begin learning the more profound lessons of ancient wisdom. The restless, aimless curiosity of the monkey starts to pursue *dharmic* satisfaction.

When our monkey calms down, energy is released, clarity comes and our consciousness changes.

Changing Consciousness

When we focus on a meditation object (whether the breath, body or a particular thought) our meditation is marked by concentration, and all our senses are harnessed for the suspension from regular operation. We can begin this process by closing our eyes when we meditate. As I move into an intensely concentrated mode, my sense of smell, touch, taste, and hearing seem to be turned off. Sometimes, all five body-based senses disappear. But my brain can generate vivid imaginings, as in a dream. The Buddha identified eight states of consciousness that we can experience in meditation. They are called *jhanas* in Pali (*dhyanas* in Sanskrit), which means 'meditations' but specifically refers to the different altered states of consciousness that come from a concentrated mind.

The first *jhana* shifts our minds from the meditation object to a pleasurable sense ('this is nice'). It is felt in the body and releases pent-up energy with increased pleasure. When that falls away, we enjoy a greater clarity of thought and an enhanced ability to examine problems and ideas. It is this concentrated consciousness that enabled Gotama to awaken fully. In this state of mind, *vipassana* (insight) thrives.

The second *jhana* refines the joyful sense of physical pleasure. It becomes less intense, but, in a sense, goes deeper. At this point, reasoned thought disappears and is replaced by intuition (an immediate sense of reality).

With the third *jhana*, pleasure morphs into contentment with a more general awareness. Our concentration both strengthens and quietens. Christians might recall the quiet exaltation of the mystic Julien of Norwich: "All shall be well, and all manner of things shall be well."[136]

The fourth *jhana* is marked by an all-encompassing equanimity. Words are not able to describe this feeling, which is without any conscious thought. The Buddha described it as resting by a lake on a hot day after a long, pleasurable swim.

These four are said to be the *rupa jhanas*, meaning they are experienced with a bodily sense. But they can lead us to a near out-of-body experience (*arupa jhanas*, formless *jhanas*). This level often progresses from the previous four, but a meditator can experience them without that, suddenly and without 'progression'.

They convey a mystical sense of experiencing ultimate reality. But this is a subjective, not objective experience, deepening the sense of calm (*samatha*) we experience in meditation. It is not true insight (*vipassana*).

Gotama's pre-awakened life included these experiences and being asked to teach them to others. He declined the invitation in order to continue his spiritual search. Even then, he saw that they were not to be equated with full Awakening. That experience was gained through the first *jhana*. It allows us to use reason, emotion, and intuition.

Some describe the formless *arupa jhanas* as four different changes experienced sequentially. Others, including myself, take them as various aspects or characterisations of the one consciousness. They are a sense of infinite space, of infinite consciousness, of "no-thingness" (a non-verbal feeling that nothing in the universe has a permanent, independent existence), and "neither perception nor non-perception".

The movement of *jhanas* is from a bodily sense to a physical presence towards an out-of-body awareness. The energies experienced become subtler. As the sense of bodily existence is replaced by pure consciousness, the autonomous "I" is fading. Consciousness is progressively less intrusive as the six senses (including rational thought) fade into the background. Although we don't see anything particular in the formless *arupa jhanas*, there is a general sense of luminosity.

It is fruitless to keep asking, 'Am I concentrated enough?', 'What *jhana* am I experiencing now?' or 'Where is this heading?' because to do so loses our concentration. The pleasures of these experiences and the sense of profound reality are enough to keep us going. The deeper the concentration, the less we are aware of time. Once, after what I assumed was a 30-minute meditation, the clock registered three hours after my beginning.

Some Common Meditations

Most meditation teachers start their students with the **Mindfulness of Breathing**. Everyone breathes and relies on their breath, so we all are fully equipped for this practice.

Metta (Kindness and Compassion) Meditation is many meditators favourite. There are many ways to organise this practice. A classic way to begin is to cultivate a kind attitude towards yourself. A friend, followed by someone you don't know and have no fixed emotions towards, then someone with whom you have a problematic relationship, and finally, wishing the good of all sentient beings.

A **Body Scan** provides an awareness of the different parts which comprise your materiality. It reveals where your physical stress is concentrated and prompts its release. This meditation exposes your impermanence and insubstantiality.

Open Awareness, often called Zen Meditation, cultivates mindfulness of all that is registering in your mind, sensing how everything that appears in your consciousness disappears, confirming the reality of impermanence.

Contemplation (sometimes termed **Reflection**) concentrates on considering a concept or quality of life in all aspects, especially as it relates to you personally. One example considers the qualities of full Awakening by contemplating the Buddha.

There are many other meditations (including flame, bell, and mantra meditation), some of which are unique to particular Buddhist traditions.

It is recommended that you find a meditation practice that "works" for you - but not to the exclusion of others. Each provides its distinctive benefits.

Gotama's Distinctive Mindfulness Meditation

The goal of Buddhist mindfulness moves beyond the relaxation and refreshment of *samatha* to confront our impermanence, insubstantiality, and need for radical change (*vipassana*). These two emphases for meditators were included in Gotama's approach to Awakening, for monks and laity alike.

Gotama was convinced that *sati-patthana* (The Foundations of Mindfulness),

"...is the way to purified living, by which we overcome sorrow and distress. Through it, our [unnecessary] pains and unpleasant feelings disappear, and we join the path that leads to our release from suffering (*nibbana*). How do you do it? You contemplate your body just as it is. Then, turn your attention to the feelings it generates. Do the same for your mind. Then consider what your mind is thinking, especially my teachings. These are your mind objects.

"These four emphases can be the gateway to your freedom. Consider them separately: the body in its materiality, then its sensations, then how your mind is engaging, and finally, the teachings (*dharmas*) I have given you. Put your energy into these reflections, seek clarity, and put aside worldly concerns."[137]

We begin with a sense of the breath. The resulting relaxation prepares us for concentrated (laser-focused) thought, and thus for insight. We notice the breath's impermanence, seeing it come and go without a rigidly fixed identity. Then, we consider in detail our meditation posture – how our body is positioned (and how it is moving if we are doing walking meditation).

This concentrated focus on the breath is the beginning of a more comprehensive mindfulness within this first focus. We then consider the different parts of the body, from our head-hair to our toenails, including our external and internal organs and their contents, their nature and their demise.

The second focus in this pattern is on "feelings", by which Gotama means our sense of what is experienced by our body and mind. This includes **pleasant feelings** (such as 'I love this ice-cream sandwich', 'I enjoy my friend's company'), **unpleasant feelings** (for example, 'This darned backache', 'Will the baby ever get toilet trained?!') and **neutral feelings** (the landscape we're not really experiencing, the radio programme that's on when you're not listening, the stranger passing us unnoticed).

For *Satipatthana's* third focus we evaluate our consciousness, contemplating the mind: Is it inclined to lust? To anxiety? To hatred? To freedom? Is it distracted or centred? As with each of these foci, we can sense the Impermanence and Insubstantiality of our minds.

The final focus is to consider "mind-objects" – specifically the elements of the *dharma,* such as some particular aspect of the Eightfold Path, the Four Ennobling Realities, or any other teaching (and the reality behind its words).

Gotama concludes his discourse by saying, "Whoever will practice these four foci (he calls them 'foundations') will become fully awakened, or close to it."

Of course, Awakening does not happen automatically by going through the motions of these exercises. If we engage honestly and sincerely with them, our full Awakening could take seven years or a week. Our personality and our preparation (knowledge and behaviour) make a difference. As with all the recommended practices, we need not adopt it until we are ready.

Begin Where You Are

Granting the Buddhist conviction that "ignorance" is the over-arching impediment to our Awakening, it's wise to master the basics before attempting the ultimate. We learn to walk before we run. And there is no shame in not joining the meditation Olympics until ready. But, continuing the metaphor, we need to keep training and nurture our aspiration to gain the goal. Thankfully, we don't have to beat any competitors. We need to develop the skills and strengths required for the final race. In terms of meditation, this means we choose a practice that suits our level of development. But we need to avoid getting stuck there.

Transformational learning has to be understood and adapted to our circumstances, particularly our readiness to receive the intended outcome. Each step in our spiritual growth builds on our previous knowledge and readiness to change. For example, if we cannot see that we generate needless suffering, we will never find a way to reverse it. If we have a negative sense of our worth, we will inevitably have a distorted understanding of self and 'no self', which will block our progress.

The Wind Beneath Our Wings

Whatever we experience or hope for meditation, we should not underestimate its importance and potential benefits. It can contribute to a calm, clear consciousness that will help us sail through both stormy times when forward movement seems impossible. Meditation can energise and empower us to sustain and support our efforts in a way that multiplies our ability to achieve the contentment we long for. It is one of the most effective ways to develop mindfulness throughout the day, strengthen our ability to concentrate, and relieve the near-inevitable stresses of 21st-century living. If the *dharma* provides a map to our Awakening, meditation can be the wind that sustains that journey.

Over to You!

1. Have you any questions about Buddhist meditation that prevent your full-hearted practice?

2. What meditation pattern(s) appeal to you most? Why?

3. Have you organised your life to facilitate a regular meditation practice?

A Secular Buddhist Spirituality

Refection: A Glorious Moment

Lotus Flower*[138]

*The Lotus is a Buddhist symbol of our human potential (Buddha Nature), with roots in the mud, nurtured by the sun, growing to perfection.

12.
A Positive Psychology

"Some consider the Buddha, who lived 2,500 years ago, to have been the first psychologist to walk the planet. While many think of Buddhism as primarily a religion, it is also a form of psychology that is consistent with the scientific method that stresses observation and judging for oneself (versus simply following dogma) ... Buddhist Psychology theory believes our psychological state depends not so much on our particular circumstances, but more on how we relate to what life brings our way."
Healthy Psychology website[139]

"In recent years, ideas drawn from the Buddhist tradition have found their way into Western psychology, informing new ways of understanding and promoting human well-being."
Seth Zuihō Segall[140]

Understanding How We Function

Just as our bodies are continuously modifying, the same is true with our minds. At every moment, we are a dynamic (impermanent) set of experiences. Thus, we have no unchanging, essential self or 'soul'. Since we are inescapably changing, we can consciously use this process as a sailor harnesses the wind. The goal is the change for the better. To do this, we need to know what needs changing.

Gotama's genius was to name the process which brings our experiences into consciousness. He has not given us a foolproof science of consciousness. Rather, his analysis alerts us, as it did his first followers, to be aware of the inherent subjectivity and complexity of our conscious awareness. He described how we develop our conscious thoughts as the "Five Clusters" (*skandha* in Sanskrit—*khanda* in Pali)[141]. These represent five different processes that happen in our experience. The metaphor is a pile of wheat or grass, with many strands in each bundle. Gotama had no knowledge of how exactly these clusters operated, but he identified the broad process in a way that suited his teaching others to know themselves so they could free themselves.

"Monks, when you think of yourself, whether you consider your material form, your feelings, your perceptions, your volitional formations, or your consciousness, see it all as it really is.

"This holds for everything. It doesn't matter if it's past, present or future, far or near, internal or external, gross or subtle, of low or excellent repute — everything should be seen as it really is.

> "So, you need to understand every part of your experience with this insight: This is not mine, I am not this, this is not my 'self'."[142]

Describing the Five Clusters Process

We'll begin by describing what the five clusters (*skandhas*) represent. Then we'll clarify how they function by simplifying the process (experience to consciousness) with two simplistic examples.

The first is **form** (*rupa*). I come against something which registers in me, through my five senses or my mind (also considered a 'sense' by Gotama). It might be a 'thing' such as another person, an object, or a thought. This first experience happens below our conscious awareness, as do the next three clusters.

This elicits a **feeling** (*vedana*). I instinctively react to this 'form' with a sense of attraction ('I like' or 'I want'), aversion ('I do not like' or 'I do not want'), or indifference (a neutral reaction that sees no good or harm – hardly noticing it).

The feeling prompts us to label the source of this experience with a particular **perception** (*samjna*). It thus registers with us with a sense of what it is, whether we really understand it or not.

We build on this foundational impression with **elaborations** (*sankhara)*), attributing many qualities and stories to it.

Finally, out this sense of the experience enters our **consciousness** (*vijnana*).

As you review this process you can see how subjective it is. Hopefully, my two examples below will prompt your own.

An Encounter with Spiders

A vivid memory from my childhood is seeing a rather large, spider when I was alone in the basement of my family home. I was around eight years old. I'm not sure what I was doing, perhaps repairing my bike, when I saw the scary, hairy-legged arachnid. He was close and closing in, ready (it seemed) to creep up my leg. I screamed. For a moment I froze. Then I ran upstairs and closed the door firmly.

Using the Five Clusters analysis, we could describe what happened as:

1. Form: I made visual contact with the spider.

2. Feeling: Instantly, I reacted with a negative feeling – a fear of spiders.

3. Perception: I sensed that it is going to/able to hurt me.

4. Elaboration: I assumed that spiders are harmful, powerful, perhaps poisonous, and out to get me.

5. Consciousness: After freezing for what seemed a very long few seconds, all the above flooded into my consciousness. I ran from the little creature.

Thankfully, I've become able to see this fear for what it is – just a fear, not a reality. Now, I live with spiders on a live-and-let-live, basis.

Facing Sudden Death

A second example relates to an incident in Chicago, during the height of the Cold War threat of a nuclear exchange between the USA and the USSR. I was a young adult working for a group called Turn Toward Peace. We were leading an effort to gain signatures in support of a test ban treaty to slow the nuclear arms race.

This story is about Larry, an accountant who, like so many, saw the threat of a war between the superpowers as a real possibility. Larry's concern led him to volunteer with our project. One day, around noon, the sirens that would be used to warn of incoming missiles sounded in downtown Chicago. We never learned why. Perhaps it was testing their functionality, or maybe a mistake.

The following weekend, I met Larry, who said something I've remembered for sixty years: "I thought it was really happening. I was relieved. The way my life is going… well, I was glad to have it end." He was facing an unexpected and unwanted divorce, and his business wasn't going well, he confided, "Best to have an end of it."

Skandha Analysis

How might we describe Larry's reaction in terms of the Five Clusters analysis (a theoretical exercise, admittedly). First, Larry heard the sirens (**form**), He experienced this sound with raw emotion (**feeling**). He was confronted with what felt like the imminent end to his life ('This is it. I'm going to die.') These were the actual words he said to me, as I recall (a false conclusion, but it was his **perception**).

Then it gets interesting, by taking an unexpected twist. Larry felt intensely the pain and hopelessness of his personal life, his split with his wife and his problems at work. He connected with his need to escape his pain. 'This will end my troubles.' The **elaboration** pulled him into a new direction. A sense of relief flooded into his consciousness based on the ultimate solution of atomic destruction. His life wasn't working, and he was glad it would be vaporised. Such was his **consciousness**.

Larry's experience and mine seemed to us 'objective'. There was a siren and a spider. But our unconscious response and then our consciousness reactivity expressed a subjective and unverifiable interpretation of its meaning. Neither Larry nor I had *skandha* analysis to understand his welcoming the bomb and I fleeing the spider. If good friends were present at the time, we might have been alerted to see our reactivity with greater clarity – that it was driven by emotion rather than reason. This could have led to insights and actions that would pour kindness and compassion on his wounds and evaluate his situation more realistically. His marriage and work difficulties could be faced and might have been resolved. I could continue repairing my bike.

The *skandhas* are not immediately apparent to our conscious thinking. But the wider Buddhist mind training prepares us for this fruitful work. Of course, this idealised story has all the answers spelt out. When we probe an experience, it often contains ambiguities and mysteries underneath our conscious understanding However, I have found *skandha* analysis a very helpful tool for getting in touch with the feelings behind my conscious thoughts, often prompting me to re-evaluate them, with positive consequences.

Of course, once a thought-feeling enters our consciousness, it doesn't disappear. And the preconscious assumptions we have are with us. Around four or five centuries after Gotama's death, the Yogacara/Yogachara tradition formed. The Yogacara monks developed a theory to explain the beliefs and experiences we store below our consciousness, which we bring to our ongoing experience. They called it 'storehouse consciousnesses' (*alayavijnana*) and discussed it as a seedbank of *karmic* actions which will draw consequences for our present or future. We can relate it to Freud's idea of the unconscious mind, which stores our experiences and determines so much of our living.

Understanding Ourselves

These two stories will, I hope, stimulate you to reflect on how you have processed your experience. The point is not to isolate the objective truth of each happening, but to consider how we perceive situations based on our initial reactions, which are shaped below our consciousness's radar. These preconscious determinations are not necessarily connected to our values and sense of reality. They are uninformed by the *dharma*. They are subjective, not objective, and often need correcting.

Meditation trains us to be aware of thoughts and feelings we have not been noticing. This awareness can be harnessed to interrogate our own minds. Our initial reactions to people and events might well be quite erroneous. I have found it extremely helpful to ask myself what lies behind strong reactive thoughts, and then to quiet my mind (avoiding rationalisations) and wait for an answer. Often, I realise that they come from a gut feeling that might well be (or obviously is) inaccurate and inappropriate. I can see how such feelings can lead me astray from the path I initially wanted to follow, especially when I bring to mind my ideals and resolutions.

We pick up the rules and assumptions from parents, peers, and the wider society. They can shape us at the subconscious level to experience life according to their orientation. This can be for good or for ill. But until we start interrogating our reactive feelings and thoughts, we will not be able to evaluate them when they occur. Socrates, a contemporary of Gotama, is quoted as saying during his trial, when accused of corrupting youth by leading them away from mindlessly accepting the social consensus, that "the unexamined life" is just as faulty. A Five Clusters consciousness can help us avoid unthinking responses that could well be dangerous, foolish, and utterly incapable of supporting the life we want for ourselves.

A Buddhist Personality Test

Today, in the search for self-understanding, we can access a wide variety of personality tests. Buddhism includes an ancient example that has proved helpful to some. In a book titled *The Path to Purity* (*Visuddhimaga*), a leading monk named Buddhaghosa (living in Sixth Century CE Sri Lanka) described an early Buddhist personality test. He described three unwholesome temperaments and showed how their energies could become wholesome forces. The unwholesome impulses are greed, aversion, and ignorance. Each unskilful motive contains within it, often masked, a transformative potential that is a great virtue, holding the possibility of behaviours that promote Awakening. This ancient pattern has been largely ignored in contemporary Buddhism, but some are using it as a tool for personal development.

As we explore our dissatisfaction, we can see the opportunities for shifting our thoughts and actions for positive outcomes. "Greed" (*lobha*) can become a hunger and thirst for what will truly benefit us and others. "Aversion" (*moha*) can be exchanged for wisdom and love, in all its dimensions. "Ignorance" (*dosa*) can be replaced by realism and curiosity.

There are simple questionnaires now available to help us to see whether our personalities are oriented towards the greed, aversion, or ignorance types.[143]

The Main Motive

Whether it's through the "psychology" of the Five Clusters Analysis, the "philosophy" of the Three Characteristics of Existence, or the "pragmatism" of the Four Realities, the aim of Gotama's teaching was a transformation that would remove all unnecessary suffering and self-preoccupation, freeing our humanity to express love for others and themselves – shifting our ego-centred consciousness to an open, constructive experience (reconstructive). This positive and lasting change begins in the mind and results in visible action.

These changes have been described in Jack Kornfield's *The Wise Heart* and have been illustrated on the Healthy Psych website.[144] Our reactive tendencies yield unskilful and painful responses, such as:

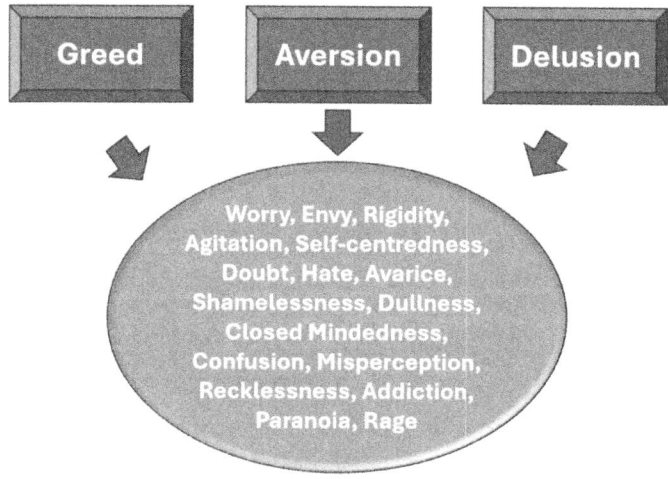

However, our mindful, skilful responses have the opposite effect. Thus:

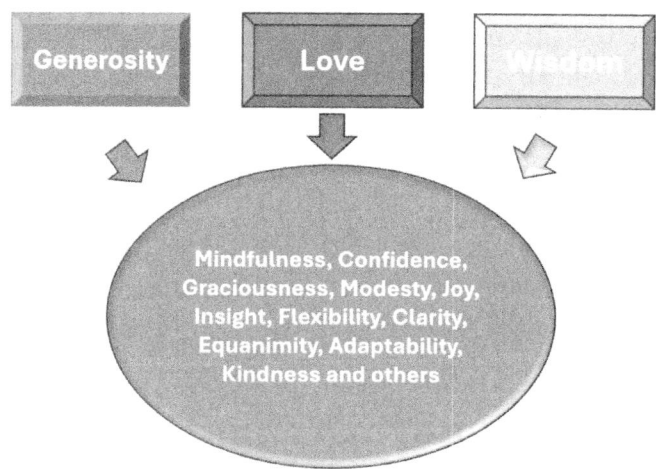

A New Stability

In the *Mangala Sutta*[145] (Blessings) Gotama lists the "greatest blessings" in life. These included wisdom, generosity, responsibility, humility, discipline, ethical living, self-restraint, patience, and "a mind unruffled by the vagaries of fortune".

After his death, this last phrase was clarified by *sutta* commentators as referring to the vicissitudes of life: the changes in our situation which can undermine the happiness of those who do not understand the *dharma*. Later, they were described as the "Eight Worldly Winds" which can blow away our equanimity and thus our inner peace. The worldly winds or *loka-dhamma* depict realities that may come to anyone on earth. They are grouped in four pairs: Pleasure and Pain, Gain and Loss, Praise and Blame, and Fame and Disrepute.

Every person, wicked or wise, skilful or unskilful, is vulnerable to changing circumstance. Sometimes it represents our past catching up with us (*karma*). But reversals of circumstance can be caused by circumstances wholly beyond our control and unrelated to our intentions. Gotama, the supreme example of an enlightened human, was free from such upheavals – but not in the sense that they never happened. Towards the end of his life, he was in extreme pain. He lost some of his closest disciples through death, but also because they became disillusioned with him. Not everyone recognised his excellence and dismissed his teachings as erroneous.

No doubt each of us can think back on some storm-tossed living in which our favourable situations were reversed. In some cases, the appropriate response might have been to make a great effort to regain our former blessings. But it is not possible. As well we might find that pleasures, gains, praise, and fame of our former lives were blocking the way to a better kind of living. Gotama suspected as much when he left his princely role and searched for a more satisfying life.

A Window on Our "Emptiness"

The Discourse on the Heart of the Perfection of Wisdom (*Prajnaparamitahridaya Sutra*), composed by an anonymous disciple long after the Buddha's death, has a unique perspective on the fluidity of the human consciousness. It states that each of the clusters are "empty" (void of a fixed existence). It begins:

The Bodhisattva of Compassion, when he meditated deeply, saw the emptiness of all five *skandhas*. This sliced through the bonds that caused him suffering. Form is nothing more than emptiness. Emptiness is nothing more than form. Feeling, perception, elaboration, and consciousness, are the same as form...[146]

The way we process all our senses reflects the fluidity of no-self. Like the objects of my perception (form), every element of our processing is impermanent (*anatta*) and thus without fixed identity (*anicca*). It is one thing to affirm the concept in the abstract, and quite different to identify your 'self' on these understandings! To see this (which can be aided by reflection on the *skandha*), frees us from unnecessary suffering. Before I came to this realisation, I would have guessed it would disturb my emotions and even devastate my confidence. But I found it a joyful thing, undercutting suffering with the joy of *dharmic* freedom, that all my 'natural' and habitual responses can be altered.

This is the essential perspective of the Four Realities (Noble Truths): so much of our suffering is created by our reactivity. It can be removed from our lives, once we understand how to do it. Gotama's multifold path to Awakening culminates in self-transcendence. A key to our ultimate peace of mind is to 'get over yourself' as a fixed entity and to free yourself from the constraints of your conditioning. This is the path to contentment.

Over to You!

1. How might a Five Cluster analysis of your attitudes and views help you with your development?

2. Can this framework help you understand or be more considerate of other people?

3. Would you find a Buddhist personality test helpful?

Reflection: Walking By

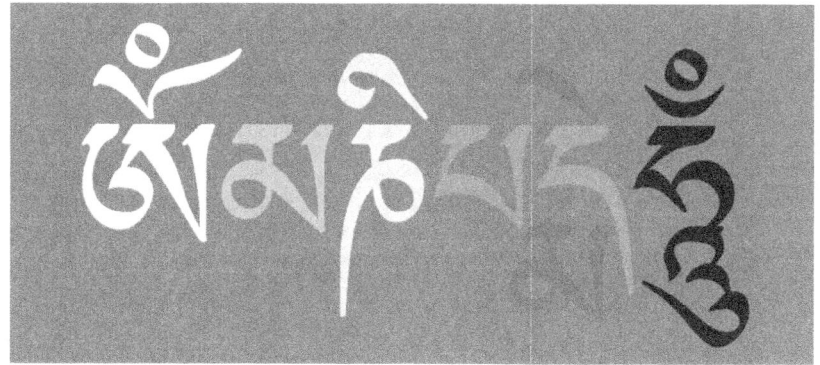

"Om ma ni pad me hum" Tibetan Mantra[147]*

*This mantra is the most loved in Tibetan Buddhism. One interpretation of its six symbols is "Praise to the jewel in the lotus". These six syllables are said to represent six perfections of Buddhist living: generosity, ethics, patience, diligence, renunciation, and wisdom.[148]

13.
Character Development

"In classical Mahayana Buddhism, the Six Perfections (*paramita*) define the meaning of human enlightenment. Buddhist enlightenment is understood to be a particular way... of being in which six distinct dimensions of human character have been cultivated to the level of excellence-generosity, morality, tolerance, energy, meditation, and wisdom."[149]

"Buddhists have maintained that nothing is more important than developing the freedom implied in their activity of self-cultivation. For Buddhists [The cultivation of character] is the primary responsibility and opportunity that human beings have."
Dale S. Wright[150]

"Character is doing the right thing when nobody's looking. There are too many people who think that the only thing that's right is to get by, and the only thing that's wrong is to get caught."
J. C. Watts, Jr[151]

"My religion is very simple. My religion is kindness."
14th Dalai Lama[152]

Character Building

Gotama's path to freedom includes an ethical self-consciousness which, if we continue with it, develops into an unconscious pattern of appropriate speech and action. Rather than doing or saying things to deliberately seek social or divine approval we just "do the right thing" as a natural expression of who we are. In Buddhist thought, ethical living puts us in touch with our greatest possible potential.

Gotama's *dharma* was a prescription for character-building. The *Cambridge Dictionary* describes character building as "helping to make someone emotionally stronger, more independent, and better at dealing with problems." From a Buddhist perspective, the most significant contribution to this development is losing the grip of our reactive self, expressed in aversion, attraction and confusion.

Like many other spiritual adepts, he taught a different way of life than was generally recognised as the road to happiness (wealth and power). He prioritised who we are (*being*) over possessions (*having*) and accomplishments (*doing*).

Character is the ultimate manifestation of virtue, as so many affirm in our modern context:

> "Human greatness does not lie in wealth or power but in character and goodness." Anne Frank

> "Lose your wealth, you lose nothing. Lose your health, you lose something. Lose your character, you lose everything." Billy Graham

"Be more concerned with character than reputation. Reputation is what people think you are. Character is what you are." John Wooden, UCLA Basketball Coach

New Habits for a Renewed You

Our ethical and spiritual growth begins in our minds, but it does not stop there:

> "Watch your thoughts, they become your words.
> Watch your words, they become your actions.
> Watch your actions, they become your habits;.
> Watch your habits, they become your character.
> Watch your character, it becomes your destiny." [153]

Gotama would have agreed.

An improved character begins with improving our intentions, but intentions without action are just daydreams. Once we determine skilful actions, we can work to make them consistent, until they become spontaneous and habitual.

One beneficial habit is to take immediate action once a genuine need or opportunity reveals itself. If we think we don't have time, we can at least note and schedule what we intend to do.

Another habit to embed in our lives is to accomplish large and complex objectives by taking smaller actions that progress towards their accomplishment, little by little. This will lead to many encouraging and satisfying results, which reinforce continuing this behaviour. "Mile by mile, it's a trial; yard by yard, it's hard; but inch by inch it's a cinch."[154]

Most Buddhists find that finding a habitual time for meditation has contributed significantly to their development of mindfulness throughout the day. My own morning routine helps me to clear my monkey mind and begin my day with a calm confidence.

Over time (with much experimentation and verification), we can renew ourselves through skilful habits. This may be the most effective strategy for becoming the person we want to be. As Gotama explained to his best friend Ananda, appropriate thoughts and actions bring joy as they release their "remorse" (their extreme discomfort when they realise the damage they have done).

Replacing Unskilful Habits

The desired change often starts with a sense that we have an inappropriate habit. We then intentionally develop a skilful pattern to replace it. This removes an immense burden from our shoulders.

I saw my need to respond to others with supportive and empathic speech when I realised the effect of my habit of "playful" sarcasm. One day I experienced discomfort when someone spoke that way to me. Later I reflected that the discomfort I experienced might be the same for those to whom I directed my own sarcastic remarks. Perhaps it was not as 'all in good fun' as I'd assumed. I began to see the passive aggression behind much of my words and consciously began a long journey of replacing sarcasm with affirmation and appreciation.

A young man, whom we'll call Martin, wanted to stop following an inner voice that advised him to "back off – it's too hard" whenever he encountered something that seemed difficult or confusing. Reading Marie Forleo's advice in *Everything is Figureoutable*,[155] Martin gained the confidence to take on the challenges he really wanted to face. He articulated a new personal mantra, "I can do this!" and used it so often it became a habit. This increased his functionality and his self-esteem.

In self-development circles, it is often stated that new habits can be developed in about three weeks (21 days of consistent practise). But, in my experience, three months or more is often required before I find it natural to act differently. Scientific studies concur. A health psychology researcher at University College London followed 96 people who wanted to develop a new habit. The average time between starting a new behaviour and doing it automatically was 66 days.[156] Regardless of the timescales involved, it's important to keep in mind that we can exchange unwholesome habits for much better ones.

Compassion Begins at Home

It is difficult to sustain positive behaviours if we do not sense a basic kindness and compassion for ourselves. This is the familiar "airline principle": in an emergency, put on your oxygen mask before you try to help other people. This counters the common misapprehension that a vigilant kindness and compassion for ourselves is "selfish". Rather, it's a key spiritual principle, and simple common sense!

I was once told to follow the JOY formula: Jesus first, then Others, and last, Yourself. But we miss something crucial when we minimise or ignore our own needs. This is not Gotama's approach. Buddhist wisdom is that we need to experience love if we are to love others. Thus, the ideal of being concerned about "all sentient beings" requires a healthy practice of self-love. Even when we feel we need to give our all to others, it is beneficial to keep at least some of the love for ourselves. At times it might seem that we've got no energy left to give to others. But usually, we can be concerned for others in our heart-mind, even when we feel unable to engage much with them.

One practice I find never fails is to 'recharge my battery' by consciously adopting a kindness and compassion mindset while out walking. This includes a smile and greeting for everyone I meet. Some may be distrustful, and others may be so preoccupied that they don't seem to notice. But most seem to welcome this positive contact – which seems to uplist both them and me. When my goodwill is not returned, I get to learn a few more lessons more about how I experience such mild disappointments.

Free Agency and Dependency

Buddhism assumes free agency. Our lives are impacted by many factors, yet we still can make individual choices that build our character. It is healthy to join the freedom of our autonomy with a concern to be helpful to others, not just to ourselves. Otherwise, we might be led by our attractions and aversions without mitigation.

Few of us are wholly independent of outside influences. We can feel we're in charge of our decisions, following all our principles, when in reality we are under the influence of social norms and parental conditioning. For example, Gotama accepted men and women from the four castes which divided society in his day. But there is evidence that he was hesitant to ordain women.[157] When he was persuaded to do so, he established rules which placed ordained women in subordination to monks. The wisest and most experienced nun had to acquiesce to the most junior monk! He seems to have been influenced by the culture of his time. Perhaps he was accommodating the prejudices of those in his movement or simply reflecting the wider social consensus.

After his death, many *sanghas* regressed to a men-only ordination and in some cultures to caste divisions.[158] Despite Gotama's opposition to a hierarchical system, his followers soon adopted a top-down leadership. This remains prevalent in many Buddhist traditions today. Perhaps it's a necessary accommodation to human nature. But it can be replaced by freer structures, as exemplified by the emergent lay communities which are developing in our time.

Choose the Best Approach for You

Buddhism has a way of providing fresh understandings of established 'common sense' concepts. Many Buddhists, follow Gotama's Middle Way teaching as a key to shaping their authentic character development.

Gotama opposed an uncritical affirmation of traditions, scriptures, and leaders. The core teachings are not meant to prompt our loyal agreement so much as to consider whether and how they might be helpful. We do well to assess how appropriate they are to our situation, mindful of our personal experience. He also warned us that "rules and rituals" can be fetters (strait jackets) that prevent our spiritual growth.

Just following Buddhist ethical and devotional practices to the letter doesn't lead to Awakening or personal virtue. We might begin our Buddhist life with a desire to live just like Gotama and his monks – and this certainly may be the right thing for a few. But it is healthy to be open to evaluating our understandings and practices to suit our twenty-first century knowledge, assumptions, and values. In every century individuals have had to determine whether and how the teaching applies to them.

Strive for Six 'Perfections'

Some centuries after Gotama's death, the Mahayana Movement promoted a renewed application of his intent – to refocus and revitalise the Buddhist community. To do so, they articulated six virtues to be pursued to perfection (*paramita*). Each was crucial for Awakening, and thus for character development. The list found in Sanskrit and Tibetan Scriptures is as follows:

1. Generosity (*dana paramita*)
2. Moral Discipline (*sila paramita*)
3. Patience (*kshanti paramita*)
4. Vigor (*virya paramita*)
5. Meditative concentration (*dhyana paramita*)
6. Wisdom (*prajna paramita*)

The Six Perfections share the same purpose as the Eightfold Path (Awakening) and are meant to energise that journey. Each perfection can be contemplated in our meditation and developed through our mindfulness and actions.

Pursuing a Multi-faceted Love

Nothing is clearer than the primacy of love for character development. The Buddha had his unique analysis of what love can mean, which he expressed in the Four Immeasurables.

The first Immeasurable is **Loving-kindness** or simply **Kindness** (*metta*) which is, well-wishing. The poetic Discourse on Loving-kindness (*Metta Sutta*) includes these thoughts:

> Whoever seeks their own welfare
> should cultivate these wishes
> for all creatures, without exception,
> weak and strong,
> visible and invisible,
> living far or near.

A second is **Compassion** (*karuna*), which is empathy and concern for those who are experiencing *dukkha* in any of its many forms. It is traditionally expressed as, 'May they be comforted and healed. May they be relieved of all unnecessary suffering.'

The third Immeasurable is a wider empathic or **Empathetic Joy** (*mudita*). I think of it as the widest possible empathy, which extends way beyond compassion. For many of us it is easier to wish 'all good' for those in distress than for people who are enjoying their lives or reaping the fruit of their labours. But we are encouraged to rejoice with those who rejoice as well as weep with those who weep.[159]

The fourth Immeasurable Is **Equanimity** (*upekkha*), which can also be translated as acceptance. But don't mistake it for the soft "love" that acquiesces with whatever is. An indifferent acceptance has no energy or imagination for improvement. Loving equanimity is committed to the very best possibilities for those involved. It will acknowledge the reality of the moment while imagining and seeking something better. It reflects a courageous and energetic love that recognises the full reality of a situation with a kindly, compassionate, sympathetic response that seeks the good of all involved.

Two of the four seated Buddhas in the Kyaik Pun[160]

A fifth aspect of love, equally immeasurable, is "**Admirable Friendship**" (*kalyanamittata*)[161], which we might translate as 'spiritual friendship' since it includes wanting and supporting all possible good for your friends in the context of *dharma* priorities, with the same desire from them for you. This kind of friendship includes a mutual desire for the Awakening of each party.

When his cousin Ananda mentioned that he had come to the realisation that half of the spiritual life, lay in spiritual friendship, Gotama famously replied, "Spiritual friendship is not half the spiritual life; it is the whole of it."[162] Our development is best progressed in the context of a community which seeks to facilitate the Awakening of every member.

Over to You!

1. What are the benefits of a skilful, positive character in your life?

2. Do you see "character development" as a primary goal of your life?

3. What aspects of Buddhist ethics might support your character development?

4.

Reflection: Boots for the journey

Contentment Here and Now

Buddha, Odilon Redon[163]

14.
Living Like a Refugee

"Going for refuge marks the point where one commits oneself to taking the *dhamma*, or the Buddha's teaching, as the primary guide to one's life."
Thanissaro Bhikkhu[164]

"The three refuges in Buddhism are not hiding places, and people who ritually 'go for refuge' are not seeking to escape from anything. Rather, they are seeking support and guidance whilst they follow a challenging spiritual path."[165]

"Who is a Buddhist? Although not all Buddhists would agree with me, I would say without hesitation that a Buddhist goes for Refuge: one who commits himself to the Buddha, the *dharma*, and the *sangha* with body, speech, and mind – in other words, totally."
Sangharakshita[166]

Our Need for a Refuge

Gotama went looking for an authentic and fulfilling life, an escape from the "good life" he had inherited, with all its conventions and restraints. He dared "go forth", searching for something better, even though he was unclear what he might find. The fact that he tried a prolonged period of asceticism, so threatening to his life, indicates both his seriousness and his ignorance of the path he later discovered.

When I became familiar with his story, I could identify with the quest to be liberated from distorting social constraints and released to a more wholesome and holistic life. I did not, however, realise the 'sacrifice' that he made. In contrast I can feel a bit cowardly and uncommitted. As a householder, then a householding monk, in the affluent West my context is so different than the jungles of ancient India.

Despite the comforts and privileges of being born into post-World War II middle class America, I was questioning the assumptions and promises I had absorbed as a child. I distanced myself from the materialistic, militaristic and racist culture that arose and shared the reactive idealism of the 1960s. With many fellow 'baby boomers' I sought new approaches to established societal norms and patterns, with a stress on social justice and a more relaxed morality. Much later, Buddhism showed me how much of what I was escaping I had absorbed, expressed in habitual thoughts, attitudes, and actions. Thankfully, the *dharma* also has helped me move away from it – and sometimes when I recognise its ghostly presence, I escape it.

I see this maintaining the acuity and strength to resist the worst in my culture and this escape as akin to seeking and finding safe harbour in dangerously stormy waters. A traditional way of saying that is "going for refuge".

You might say that I (along with so many others in the 1960s) were looking for a refuge from our imperfect society - not really a 'safe' escape but a new way forward for ourselves and our nation. Those days are long gone. But given the pressures and difficulties of our times, increasing numbers of people are seeking a radical refuge, or at least exploring how best to seek it.

The Original Refuge Seekers

The earliest records show people responding to Gotama's call to Awakening with the words, "I go for refuge". They were expressing an ancient Indian assumption that we should find security and protection in a patron. Some power greater than themselves was needed for hopeful living. It could be a wealthy compatriot, a *Raj* (ruler), a god (*deva*) or a spirit who would shield them from harm and perhaps bestow favours as well.[167] Of course, such patrons expected much in return, not least loyalty and respect, and often a portion of their meagre material resources.

Gotama adapted the idea of refuge to his understanding of discipleship, which was not centred on him, but on the *dharma*. After his Awakening, he pondered the fact that he could no longer look to be led by anyone, because he had a spirituality more fully realised than all but other Buddhas. But he sensed he needed someone/something to revere, and he concluded that he would revere the *dharma* – the source of all enlightenment.

> Past Buddhas,
> future Buddhas,
> and whoever is the Buddha now,
> all have continued to revere the true *dhamma*.
> This, for Buddhas, is a natural law.[168]

When the early Buddhists sought their refuge in the Buddha, they were not seeking Gotama as a patron, but teacher who pointed to something beyond himself (the *dharma)*. If we too follow its reality to its end, we too will become Buddhas. Thus, the salvation he offered was not a patron's gift but instruction and support for their work to Awaken. The effort required may be great, but the benefits are immense.

When the merchants Tapussa and Bhallika saw Gotama the week after his enlightenment, they shared their meal with him (rice cakes and honey). His presence and conversation were so striking that they perhaps responded impulsively, "We go for refuge to the Buddha and the *dharma*. Beginning from today, let the blessed one consider us his followers for as long as we have breath."[169]

A similar example is found in Yasa's story. He was the pampered son of a rich merchant and became disillusioned with his life of youthful sensual indulgence. Yasa went to the Buddha to discover a better way. Discerning his sincerity, Gotama shared the understanding of "suffering, its origin, its cessation, and the path to its cessation." Then Yasa's father came to him, concerned about his son. He too was ready for the *dharma*. After hearing Gotama's teaching, he went for refuge and Yasa responded similarly. When a large group of Yasa's young associates came to see what had happened to their friend, many followed in his footsteps.[170]

The early scriptures present these responses in terms of a formula: "I go to the Blessed One for refuge and to the *dhamma* [*dharma*] and to the *sangha* ..."[171] Once the movement began growing, Going for Refuge seemed to be the expected response when people embraced Gotama's teaching. Later, perhaps, it became a liturgical formula.

A Triple Affirmation

The Going for Refuge formula has been repeated for millennia when Buddhists gather in formal *sangha* meetings. It is repeated three times to stress its importance and underscore the seriousness of its implied discipleship:

> *Buddham saranam gacchami*
> I go to the Buddha for refuge.
> *Dhammam saranam gacchami*
> I go to the *dhamma* for refuge.
> *Sangham saranam gacchami*
> I go to the *sangha* for refuge.
>
> *Dutiyampi Buddham saranam gacchami*
> For a second time, I go to the Buddha for refuge.
> *Dutiyampi Dhammam saranam gacchami*
> For a second time, I go to the *dhamma* for refuge.
> *Dutiyampi Sangham saranam gacchami*
> For a second time, I go to the *sangha* for refuge.
> *Tatiyampi Buddham saranam gacchami*
> For a third time…

In our Scottish Centre for Pragmatic Buddhism, we use a modified version of this ritual:

> This very day, I go for my refuge to the Three Jewels:
> to the Buddha, the consummating personal element,
> our inborn contentment,
> and to the *dharma*, the consummating teaching element,
> our dedication to lifelong learning,
> and to the *sangha*, the consummating social element,
> our source of inspiration and support.
> May I be open to all that will help me flourish!

Three-in-One

The roots of our refuge – *Buddha, dharma, sangha* – reflect a single source. We respond to Gotama's transformed life, teaching, and the community he established and nurtured. Yet, each element requires a different kind of response. We respect the Buddha and seek to imitate him. We study the *dharma*, striving to understand how it can apply to our situations. We join with the *sangha* to be part of a caring, learning community.

It is known as "the Triple Jewels" or "the Three Treasures" (three elements that reinforce one another). Each is a crucial resource for our Awakening. It would be difficult, even impossible for some, if one or two were missing.

It's Not All About Gotama

The *dharma* refuge represents what the Buddha exemplified and taught. He lay foundations which successive generations interpreted, developed, and supplemented with the best available insights. But we would be foolish to limit ourselves only to those ancient traditions.

We are faced with contemporary concerns, such as the role of citizens in a democratic society, issues of global justice, the multi-crisis of our time, or the implications of gender ambiguity and fluidity. Gotama established a framework for approaching any issue. But it would be foolish not to draw on all possible resources as we seek the common good and our own skilful engagement with the world. The insights of contemporary psychology, physics, neurology, and evolutionary theory are just a few of the resources available to us that offer important supplements to Buddhist thought.

Reliance on Gotama's moral compass and wise understandings does not deny the utility of new understandings and applications for the challenges of our time. If teachings from other sources, both ancient and modern, help us with our development, we can embrace elements of their "*dharma*" too.

In a similar vein we can widen our interpretation of the *sangha*, to learn from non-Buddhist communities. Though now a committed Buddhist, I still benefit from what I received from the community established by Ignatius Loyola (the Jesuits), my years as a Third Order Franciscan, and my time with the Presbyterians, Evangelicals, and Methodists. Although I have abandoned many of their foundational assumptions, they have given me many beneficial skills, insights and practices.

Five Moral Precepts

To take refuge in the Buddha is to live like a Buddha, as fully as possible, which includes reflecting his character. To this end, many *sanghas* include an affirmation of Five Precepts (*pancasila*) as part of Going for Refuge.

The precepts are pledges to avoid key unskilful actions that could be harmful to ourselves and others. The skilful alternatives restrain us from these behaviours. The precepts traditionally include:

- No Killing,
- No Stealing,
- No Sexual Misconduct,
- No Lying,
- No Intoxicants.

Their roots go back to Gotama's teaching, as reflected in some of the early discourses.[172]

Each of these precepts is subject to interpretation, and these can vary between different Buddhist communities. They are often influenced by distinct traditions, the cultures in which we exist, and the particular interests or emphases of the community's leadership. Some *sanghas* are quite firm, even rigid in their interpretations, while others are much looser. Within a *sangha* there can also be individual disagreements about applying the precepts.

For some No Killing (the first precept), can mean 'no unlawful taking of life', thus allowing Buddhists to serve in the police or armed services. But it is widely understood as abstaining from taking the lives or even harming any living being. Thus, some Buddhists oppose abortion and assisted suicide as well as murder. Some are as deeply concerned for animal welfare as they are for human flourishing. A vegetarian or vegan diet is often seen as a logical extension of the no harm principle. Refraining from mind-clouding intoxicants (alcohol and drugs) is also interpreted variously, from total abstinence to moderation.

If we take the precepts as rigid rules ('laws' or 'commandments') we are missing the benefit that comes from reflecting on their ability to engage our best thinking and develop our character. We become stuck in obedience mode, which can stifle lifelong learning and moral development.

My *sangha* frames the five precepts with words that encourage individual interpretations:

1. I undertake the training of loving-kindness.
2. I undertake the training of generosity.
3. I undertake the training of moderation and contentment.
4. I undertake the training of positive speech.
5. I undertake the training of life-affirming action.

For us No Killing is implied in its positive alternatives of loving kindness and life-affirming action. No Intoxicants is covered within the wider principle of moderation.

A Fulsome Refuge

Traditionally, all Buddhists affirm the three refuges during high holidays and other significant events, such as their wedding ceremony. There is much to commend the concept of a triple refuge, over an emphasis on his person or his teaching alone. This has roots that take us back to the original movement. In one of the earliest expressions of Gotama's thoughts, the triple refuge is at the centre of our progress:

> "Whoever takes refuge in the Buddha, the *dharma*, and the *sangha* understand their dissatisfaction, its cause and termination, and how to end it. This is a secure refuge, a supreme refuge. Those who seek it find release from their sorrow."[173]

Were we to affirm only the teaching, we might easily make Buddhism a dry set of rational principles. If our refuge were only the Buddha, he might easily be seen as a living saviour who can personally solve all our problems. Should our refuge be only the *sangha*, we might find our spirituality drowning in social consensus and conviviality. But the three together make a balanced whole in which each one both moderates and supplements the others. The triple refuge (Buddhism's three-in-one formula) conveys a confidence that if we seek, and keep seeking, all three refuges, we shall have a varied source of comfort, assurance, and challenge.

In lands where Buddhism has been dominant for centuries, those raised in an extended context will almost inevitably have that identity given to them from childhood and assumed throughout their lives. For many, their 'faith' is more one of outward conformity than a transforming growth of mind and heart. We might say their Going for Refuge is cultural. Yet they are free to leave Buddhism or to become disciples on their own terms.

Whatever their context, others might engage as Buddhists with their own goal. Or they might have a very concrete (but limited) understanding of what Buddhist principles and practices can do for them. At some point, we all will encounter values and viewpoints that we consider irrelevant or intrusive. Our sense of Going for Refuge can profit by being open to a broader understanding.

Going for Refuge does not imply a perfect motive, only a sincere desire to awaken and a trust that the three refuges are the means to do it.

Seeking Refuge Makes Us Refugees

We seek refuge when we leave our cultural, spiritual, and psychological homeland. If we judge that we've found a promising alternative to our lives, we will orient our lives to the new culture. Refugees, desperate for a better, more secure life. They risk their resources and often their lives to escape their suffering. They are often misled by false expectations or the promises of others. When they find a credible path, they embrace it fully.

"I left my parents, my house, my achievements,
my friends, my job and even my ambitions that
I had worked hard to fulfil back in my country."[174]

It's far from easy being a refugee. But, if the new homeland accepts us, it can be a joyous experience – especially if it meets our deepest desires. At its best, it is a place of safety and a welcome to join a new community, with an open door to a dynamic set of opportunities – a chance to grow into our full potential. With this intention, we respond to Gotama's example, teaching, and community: "I go for my refuge…"

Over to You!

1. Is the focus on three refuges an enhancement or a hindrance to your desired growth?

2. In what sense might the Buddha, *dharma*, and *sangha* be a refuge for you?

3. What other refuges are you relying upon or seeking?

Refection: Connected

***Bodhisattva* Ksitigarbha ("Earth Store")**[175]

15.
More Than Me and Mine

"He drew a circle that shut me out:
'Heretic, rebel, a thing to flout.'
But love and I had the wit to win:
We drew a circle and took him in!"
Outwitted, Edward Markham

"Outside of self a world awaits
For love signs. - I want to see
Just beyond 'me', then can create
An easier day for other than ' I '"
Just Beyond Me, Fay Slimm

"Abandon harmfulness. Embrace skilfulness
Purify the mind...
If you harm another, you are no contemplative...
These are the teachings of all buddhas."
Dhammapada, Verses 183-184, Author's paraphrase

"A monk's practice ought to be thus: I have no self, and nothing is mine. In the future, there'll be no self, and nothing will be mine."
The Good Person's Departure (Early Chinese Buddhist Scripture), Translated by Charles Patton[176]

No-self (*anatta*)

Perhaps Gotama's most challenging wisdom is 'no-self'. We simply cannot maintain the sense of selflessness of advanced meditative states (the *jhanas*). So why is *anatta* considered so important, even essential, in Buddhism?

Essentially, no-self is meant to counter the assumption that our identity is fixed. "No fixed self" might be a clearer and less confusing way of expressing this crucial concept. It asserts that both human nature and the rest of the natural world have a changing nature, because of the realities of impermanence.

Too easily we can insist that "I've got to be me" or "I did it my way" as though my personality and nature is unalterable. Such judgments might express what we think we are; yet they reflect an ignorance of the way all things, including human beings, really are: forever changing.

No-self is a beneficial concept. It allows us to move forward without being tied to an earlier self-image. Rather than weakening our sense of personal identity, as some suppose, no-self makes us stronger with its flexibility. I can change myself for the better.

> "…The *anatta* teaching is not a doctrine of no-self, but a not-self strategy for shedding suffering by letting go of its cause, leading to the highest, undying happiness".[177]

As we place ourselves in the wider frame of each moment (being aware of external as well internal influences) we learn to exchange our erroneous thoughts with a more accurate awareness. We become more confident about what we are experiencing and how we want to respond.

Buddhists who have been practicing for years are – in my experience – clear about who they are and what they are about. Their self-knowledge assumes rightly that we all can change for the better (as expressed in the third and fourth Ennobling Realities).

An understanding of no-self facilitates our growth. Within this concept is the thought, 'If I am changing anyway (my impermanence), I might as well strive for improvement'. We and all that we relate to 'inter-are' within a reality which is much larger than an isolated individuality. This aspect of no-self enlarges our self-consciousness, rather than denying or minimising it. We are stronger for it.

Self-ish Barriers to Inner Freedom

This sense of relatedness is the way of universal peace, so needed in today's divided world. This theme expresses a desire portrayed in many popular stories, such as the film Independence Day and its sequel, Resurgence, in which the rival world powers join together to defeat a common enemy (an invasion of aliens). Buddhists see that the roots of peace come from discarding the divisive concept of me/us against all others. This realisation would help to resolve intractable hostilities between nations, communities, and individuals.

To separate our identity from others is inevitably divisive and destructive. This encourages the opposite of altruism. Inquisitions, Holocausts, Ethnic Cleansings, Invasions, Slavery, Sexual Exploitation and Misogynies of past and present centuries have showcased the worst of our selfishness, individual and collective. But such obscenities have been countered by those who oppose them: courageous men and women who were often led and sustained by a deeply humanistic spirituality.

It is easy to judge ourselves as powerless to change society or counter the powerful political, commercial, criminal, and ideological forces that are pursuing a destructive agenda, often without realising it – encouraged by their inner voices and their 'tribe'. For some, this sense of impotence leads to the conclusion that we should restrict the Buddhist life to inward activities. They equate a vital spirituality solely in terms of mindful contemplation, self-examination, and meditation. But this is a departure from both the original spirit of the movement and the forces of contemporary renewal.

The *Bodhisattva* Ideal

The ultimate expression of Buddhist spirituality is individuals setting aside one's own Awakening in order to work for the Awakening of all beings. This is known as the *Bodhisattva* Ideal.

The *Bodhisattva* Ideal is often thought to require innumerable lifetimes. But a secular, pragmatic approach focuses on many opportunities we must be a positive influence on all those we meet in the life we're living 'here and now'. Neither does it neglect our own needs. Although its desire to focus on the Awakening of all others, that ironically is extremely beneficial to our own development.

The *Bodhisattva* Ideal comes from Mahayana Buddhism which emerged to reform the increasingly self-centred focus of the monastics, whose individual practices were aimed at liberating only the practitioner. This ideal expressed the spirit of Gotama, who seemed to forget his own advantage for the sake of others – though admittedly after, not before, his enlightenment.

Shantideva, an Indian monk, scholar, and poet who lived in the 7th or 8th Century CE, wrote what many consider the best expression of this ideal in his *Guide to the Bodhisattva's Way of Life*. It advocates the cultivation of the six "perfections" (*paramita*) of Buddhism: (1) giving (2) discipline (3) patience (4) diligence (5) meditative concentration and (6) wisdom.

Shantideva realised that by perfecting ourselves, we would be living a contented life and, in the process, escaping our self-obsession. He identified anger and hate as a great enemy of Awakening, because its negativity prevents positive living and corrupts our thoughts:

Hatred destroys the possibility of peaceful sleep and waking pleasure. It wounds our hearts and destroys our security. Even if we shower our friends and relatives with gifts, they will avoid us, despise us, and discount our generosity if we have a hating heart. We are disfigured by hate. It negates all the benefits of our advantages. But when we see anger and hate as thieves who rob us of our peace, leaving only suffering, we can be happy forever.[178]

Archetypal Figures

Carl Jung introduced the term "archetype" in the early 20th century.[179] It points to human paradigms and profiles that are resonant with all humanity. Examples are the Hero, Mother, and Wise Old Man (or Woman). Such universally recognised figures influence our thoughts, behaviours and emotions, which seem to be stored in the depths of our 'collective unconscious'. Jung thought that archetypes connect with our evolutionary heritage.

Bodhisattvas can be seen as archetypes representing a deep commitment to benefit all beings (reflecting the 'altruistic gene' in every one of us).

The most prominent *Bodhisattvas* are Avalokiteshvara and Guan Shi Yin (Guanyin), Buddhist archetypal figures, representing kindness and compassion, joined with all the other qualities associated with Awakening (notably, wisdom).

With both figures, the emphasis is not just on seeing and hearing human needs but responding to them. Their supreme focus is to serve distressed human beings. One depiction of Avalokiteshvara envisions him with 1000 arms, each representing a different way of expressing kindness and compassion. In many depictions of these *bodhisattva* archetypes, they are poised to rise from their chairs as soon as they become aware of a human need.

Kuan-yan (Guanyin) *Bodhisattva*[180]

Altruism Benefits the Giver

An evolutionary view of spirituality might argue that altruism – an active concern for others' welfare – has become a genetic trait because it supports our survival. Hopefully, the 'law of the jungle' (achieving our advantage through brute force) will be replaced or supplemented by a realisation that benefitting others gives us a crucial advantage.

"Altruism is an essential aspect of our lives that can bring numerous benefits. By engaging in acts of kindness and generosity, we can promote social connection, enhance our sense of purpose, improve our mental health, and promote empathy and compassion."[181]

Altruism was articulated by the originators of the self-development movement[182] as a key beneficial behaviour. It is emphasised by many of the contemporary self-development and self-care advocates, such as Tony Robbins who argues that "The secret of living is giving."[183] And its advantages have been academically supported.[184]

Contemporary botany and biology are still discovering how this kind of cooperation is not limited to humanity.[185] Recent discoveries reveal how "Trees are linked to neighbouring trees by an underground network of fungi that resembles the neural networks in the brain."[186] Altruism may well reflect a universal natural law. Its benefits are an aspect of 'things as they really are'; no wonder that Gotama emphasised it.

Evaluating Our Impact

We can find spiritual assertions, such as the value of altruism, attractive because they prompt good feelings. But they can seem irrelevant to rational analysis and unrelated to the lives we actually live. But Leslie Zobel, a computer programmer and practicing Buddhist, shared with me a way of bringing them together. She uses a method of determining the value of a project. The following framework can be used as a planning tool before any major effort, such as considering a new role at work or any significant shift. Before launching a major initiative, we consider the positives and negatives for ourselves and others in terms of immediate and longer-term effects. After it's been running long enough to provide significant experiential data, we can determine the validity of our anticipations. This will reveal the need for modifications to the system.

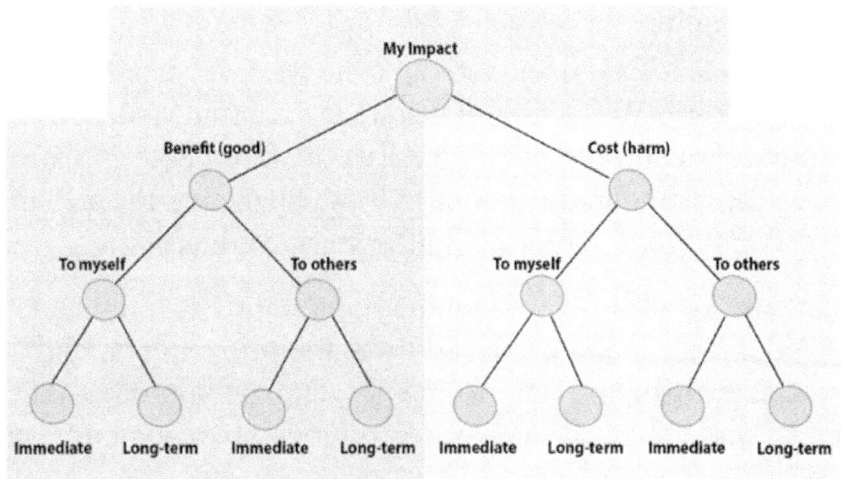

This benefit/loss analysis can be applied to Tony Robbins' framework for evaluating the use of our time (and, therefore, an aid to life planning).[187] He observes that all our decisions are made by a sense of the pleasure or pain when we consider our past and future actions. Robbins emphasises that effective decision-making requires intelligence, but also emotion. When anticipating the results of our actions, we need to be clear about the pleasure that will be gained and the pain that will be avoided by a proposed action. These positives and negatives can become emotional drivers.

Engaged with Social Needs

The wider Buddhist community is broadening its understanding of social morality. Thich Nhat Hanh offered both sides in the Vietnam war a positive alternative to its brutal violence. He coined the term "socially engaged Buddhism" – freeing morality from the hindrances of individualism and quietism, arguing that,

> "We let individualism prevail in the twentieth century, and frankly, we have made a mess of it. We must begin anew for the twenty-first century; we need a new direction. We can no longer continue destroying ourselves and the planet we live on. With determination, we can abandon the cult of individualism and the self, and act and live in harmony, in the spirit of interbeing."[188]

In many ways, we sense that the social fabric is falling apart: Democracy is being replaced by autocratic leaders; climate crises are inflicting environmental damage and devastating lives; and wars strain our resources and increase our anxieties.

Sadly, this is draining the energy and resolve for reversing such trends, leading to a cocooned existence that puts the needs of others out of reach. In contrast, we can be inspired by Thich Nhat Hahn's affirmation of an energy with elements of awareness that brings something broader than our self-contained identity to our sense of the present moment.[189] During the Vietnam war he led his monastic community out of their meditation hall into the wider community. They went out to where bombs were falling, and most of their compatriots were suffering. Their awareness of an appropriate social engagement – their connection to all those involved in the conflict, near and far – contrasts with an unengaged, passive well-wishing. The impact of this one Zen monk upon the wider Buddhist community cannot be underestimated.

Ashoka's Example of Social Concern

Buddhists point to the Indian empire builder Ashoka as a model for political leadership. Ashoka ruled most of the Indian sub-continent from 268-232 BCE, when Buddhism was the most influential religion on the Indian spiritual smorgasbord.

Referring to his last military conquest (260 BCE), Ashoka publicly admitted to slaughtering "A hundred thousand people... A hundred and fifty thousand more were deported." But in the same proclamation, under a new name, Piyadassi (translates as "he who looks with kindness on everything"), he expressed extreme remorse for all the suffering he caused. He was now devoted to the victories gained by his *dharmic* influence.[190]

Ashoka concluded with a wish for his sons and grandsons that,

> "[They] should not think of gaining new conquest, and in whatever victories they may gain should be satisfied with patience and light punishment. They should only consider conquest by *dharma* to be a true conquest. Delight in *dhamma* should be their whole delight, for this is of value in both this world and the next."

In other public edicts, Ashoka urged good behaviour in accordance with the *dharma* by all in his empire. This included avoiding cruelty to animals, even banning the killing of many species. Ashoka has become a legendary symbol of a ruler who lived an exemplary life that all his subjects could follow.

Co-operation and Compromise

The dynamic identity of every human includes their relationship with other people. Interbeing recognises our many identities, including family, interest groups, culture, religion, and nation.

Buddhism, like most spiritualities, does not prescribe a specific social blueprint but encourages people to apply their values to achieve skilful and wholesome ends at every level of the social order. That was the primary means that Gotama used for the good of society.

Cooperative joint action can make a positive difference. The 'water bucket effect' applies when our singular influence combines with others. Just as many drops can fill the bucket, many people working on the same project can make a real difference. No one has everything needed to rescue the environment, prevent war, redress past horrors, reverse present ones, and promote an increasingly just society. Most often our best chance to improve our situation (and the wider world as well) is to find and effect solutions with others. No one can do all that is required or address every need. We can sensibly limit our activities, lest we burn out.

The consciousness of our inter-relatedness can improve our character. By cooperative, appropriate action, we can find our cynicism diminishing, our courage increasing, and our understanding clarified. The non-absolutist perspective of the Middle Way can orient us to being able to seek to understand hose who come to a discussion with vastly different concerns and assumptions. The Buddhist virtue of curiosity will encourage us to listen and clarify opinions which are different from our own. The implicit humility of interbeing will cut across the confrontational and closed-mindedness that threatens our culture, even our survival, in our time.[191]

Thus, a sense of our interdependence can strengthen domestic partnerships, family life, and political dialogue. But the benefits of interbeing will not be realised if we limit it to a mystical sense and sentimental experience. Its power is released in the hurly burly of human interaction.

Many Buddhists have bailed out of the party-political process, choosing not to vote or to be informed of the choices put before the electorate. They sometimes say they just want to be *dharmic* (or spiritual). Because Gotama walked away from the responsibilities and privileges of the ruling class for something infinitely better, it could be argued that he modelled political indifference. However, Gotama was 'a man for others' to the full extent that his situation allowed.

The movement he started made India a Buddhist nation in three short centuries. It is hard to imagine that this would have happened without the integrity and effectiveness of ordained and lay *dharma* practitioners demonstrating that the Buddha's teachings could renew lives into something much better, in every aspect of their lives.[192] Gotama's ethics go way beyond mere individual concerns.

Many Charities Deserve Our Support

One of the easiest and potentially best ways of cooperating (co-operating) is through participation in charity groups. There is no shortage of these available. My online search of "Buddhist Charities" returned over four million links. But we need not constrict our giving to Buddhists only. Most of my contributions to "good works" support efforts that are not explicitly Buddhist. However, I am encouraged by the many explicit Buddhist initiatives for human betterment. The largest and most comprehensive (at the time of publishing) is Tzu Chi, "The Buddhist Compassionate Relief Charity Foundation".

Tzu Chi was founded in 1966 by a Taiwanese nun whose vision of practical *dharma* was inspired by "Chinese Humanism". Their spirituality emphasises compassionate care for people with low incomes rather than teaching and rituals. The work was initially supported by thirty Taiwanese housewives who saved 2 US cents daily to donate to needy victims of a fire that destroyed 43 homes. Their motto is "kindness, compassion, joy, and selfless giving."

Tzu Chi Logo: "Love and Faith in Action"

The Tzu Chi Foundation emphasises relief, medicine, education, and developing a humanistic culture. Ten million "members" in 47 countries support its work. In my country, the United Kingdom, Tzu Chi has volunteer hubs in six different centres. They raise money for disaster relief and refugee support, run soup kitchens, befriend older folks, and offer help for people experiencing homelessness. Elsewhere, Tzu Chi has built schools, universities, hospitals, and community centres.

Of course, many charitable efforts and organisations in the Buddhist world offer similar practical, humanistic efforts. Organisations from every faith and none are providing crucial support to those suffering throughout the world. We do well to join them, whether as financial and volunteer contributors or with neighbourly, social, and political actions. The opportunities are innumerable.

The Dark Side of Social Engagement

Unfortunately, the movement towards social engagement does not always represent goodwill and peaceful, loving actions. The travesty of ethnic and religious violence in some Buddhist nations is too well documented to ignore.[193] An example is the nationalistic Buddhist support of violence against minority peoples in Myanmar and Sri Lanka. "While largely seen as a compassionate and peaceful religion across the world, Buddhism is also a source of nationalism, extremism, and violence."[194]

So many conflicts seem driven by hatred, fear, and self-interest. In theory, this should be eradicated from Buddhist cultures by an ethically informed mindfulness, an equanimous recognition of every challenging situation, and concepts of self and *sangha* that are free from arrogant self-assertion. But history has proved how easily a sense of national or cultural identity, combined with a concern for ourselves and our social group (me and we), can lead us away from the qualities Gotama taught were necessary for individual and mutual benefit. As with every religion and ideology, a Buddhist identity does not automatically translate into absorbing and reflecting its highest ideals.

Two Wolves

Two Wolves[195]

When I introduced the concepts of skilfulness and unskilfulness in my mindfulness class, a prisoner's face lit up. He enthusiastically responded, "It's like the two wolves!" "What's that?" I asked. He was surprised I didn't know the story. He was eager to share it.

A young boy from the Cherokee nation came to his grandfather, filled with anger at someone who had done him an injustice. As he often did, his beloved 'Pa responded with a story.

"I too, at times, have felt great hate, especially when I think of all that has been taken away from our proud nation. But hate wears you down, and it hurts only you. It's like taking poison when you wish your enemy dead.

"I have come to see that there are two wolves inside us. "One is good and does not want to harm anyone. He lives in harmony with all around him and it takes no offence, even when it was intended.

"But the other wolf, is full of anger. The littlest thing will set him into a fit of temper. He fights everyone, all the time, sometimes for no reason. He can't think because his anger and hatred are so great. It leaves him helpless, because it will change nothing.

"Both of these wolves live inside me, and they compete to rule my spirit."

The boy looked intently into his Grandad's eyes and asked, "Which wolf will win?"

His Grandfather's smile was full of kindness when he replied, "The one I feed, son. The one I feed."

Once we learn to realise our unwholesome reactive patterns and their unwholesome sources, we can counter them. We learn that the "good" wolf inside us (our capability to be skilful) is much stronger than we had thought. In fact, it is stronger than its destructive sibling. As Gotama insisted, "Hatred cannot overcome hatred. Only love can do that." (*Dhammapada*, verse five)

The 'good wolf' in Buddhism is expressed in terms of our Buddha Nature. We all have the potential for wisdom and character at such a level that we, too, become Buddha (Awake). But it would be misleading to think of this energy as the only one within us and the universe. If we are to Awaken, we need to know the unskilful forces which can masquerade in sheep's clothing. Both wolf energies are not only within us. They are also in the wider universe. We need to choose what energies to welcome and cultivate.

Over to You!

1. List what you can do to make the world a better place. It might surprise you how doable some of the items are.

2. Have you experienced self-forgetfulness when relating to other people? If so, did it shrink or expand your happiness?

3. Can you think of any people who seemed to transcend their self-advantage and harmful reactivity for the good of others? If so, what can you learn from their example?

Reflection: Down

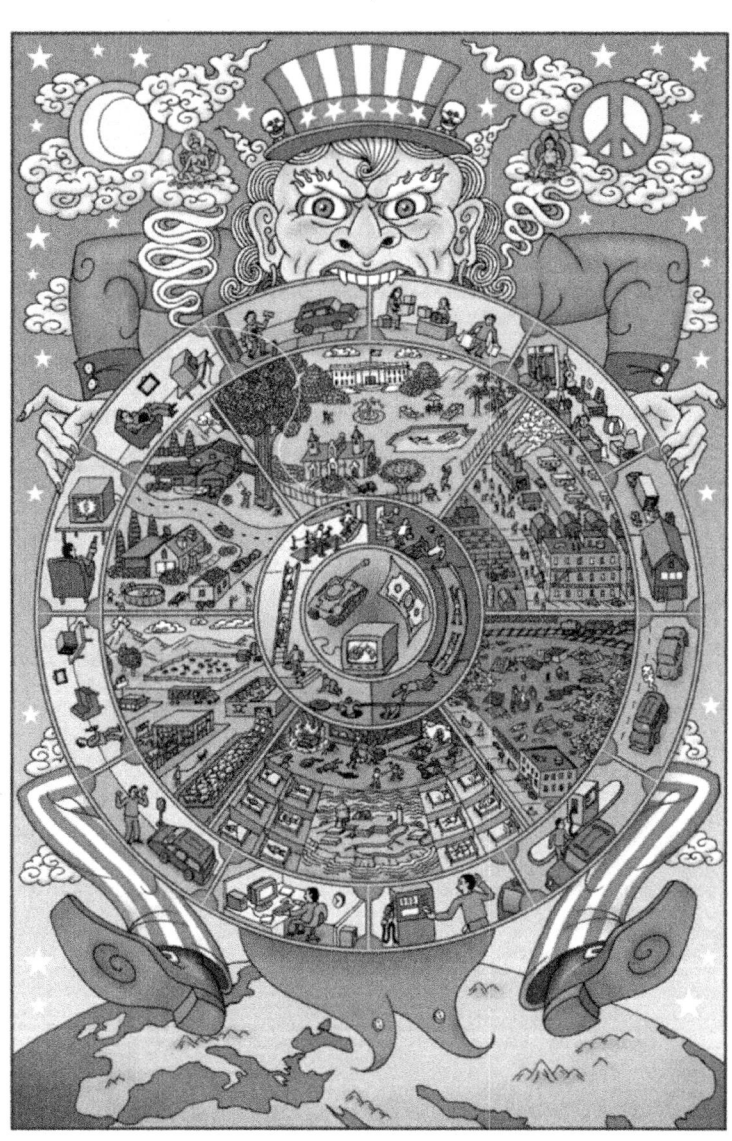

**Americosmos[196]
An American Wheel of Life**

16.
The Wheel of Life

"The Wheel of Life or Wheel of Becoming is a *mandala* - a complex picture representing the Buddhist view of the universe. To Buddhists, existence is a cycle of life, death, rebirth and suffering that they seek to escape altogether."[197]

"From a psychological perspective, the six realms can be understood as representing specific states of mind that all sentient beings experience at one time or another, each of which influences one sense of crowdedness or *dukkha*."[198]

An Educational and Motivational Mural

I am told that Tibetan Buddhist Temples and Monasteries all feature an illustrated Wheel of Life (*bhavacakka* in Pali). Its origins are Indian, from the first or second century CE. Legend has it that Gotama drew it himself to show illiterate farmers and cowherds the meaning of living without the *dharma* and the hope of a better future. In some sense, the Wheel is an expanded depiction of the first Ennobling Reality, a depiction of the many ways we can suffer. By underscoring the ultimate futility of lives without *dharma*, this visual is meant to motivate us to seek something better than being trapped in unnecessary, painful *dukkha*.

Many individuals have smaller versions of this Wheel painted on cotton or silk, making its message a vital presence in Buddhist homes. There are numerous variations in the wheel's design (according to the traditions that promote it), with minor differences that highlight specific understandings.

The Wheel of Life depicts the many ways we experience *samsara* (living in the world without a knowledge of our Buddha Nature and its potential). We might call it the unawakened life or life before liberation. This visual sermon is meant to confront us with the need to transcend all the worldly mindsets that trap us in various kinds of suffering. If and as we identify with any part of it, we are encouraged to consider a better way to think and act.

Although the Wheel of Life does not offer specific instructions about how to awaken, it provides many hints concerning the hope the Buddha offers us.

A Tibetan Wheel of Life[199]

Four Circles, Two Energies

The Wheel of Life is a mandala[200] that consists of four concentric circles (populated with illustrative characters), with some symbolic figures beyond them all. The outer circle contains twelve elements, under it is another divided into six. The next circle has two sections, and the innermost circle contains three figures.

A Buddha or *bodhisattva* figure is present at the top and in each of the third circle's six divisions.

Above the four circles, we can see depictions of two contrasting energies.

The first, the monster Yama, is a demon of impermanence, embracing all the circles. His name signifies Death. In his inescapable grip he holds *samsara*: endless suffering caused by our repeated patterns of unskilfulness, encouraged by short-sighted values. Yama speaks to our deep subconscious, which fears both death and judgment.

The second energy is the Buddha's. He assures us that we have hope if we grasp it and follow his *dharma*. We can come to embrace change. It is an undeniable fact and allows positive changes. We need not be stuck in the painful situations shown in the Wheel. We can take action to better our situation and thus escape *samsara*.

The path out of *samsara* is indicated at the top of the Wheel. The Buddha points to the moon (symbolising the Awakened life in its complexity and mystery). Awakening is a force more powerful than *samsara*.

A finger pointing to the moon[201]

The Innermost Circle

The three animals pictured at the hub of the Wheel represent the Three Poisons. The cockerel symbolises greed, the snake speaks of hatred, and the pig represents ignorance and self-delusion. These forces confront our natural energies of equanimity, compassion, and wisdom. The poisons combine to suppress our natural inclination for spiritual growth. They are primitive forces within us which can be transformed, by the *dharma*.

The inner circle asks everyone who sees it, 'What dynamic is driving you?' Greed and hatred are relatively easy to identify. We can see how other people can easily be led by ignorance (such as supposed racial or social superiority). But our tendency to self-delusion often clouds our consciousness.[202]

The Second Circle

We are then confronted by the consequences of our actions (*karma-phala*). On the left, we move upwards towards our goal; on the right, we descend from what we sought, dragged by a *dharma* guardian who won't let us get away from our just desserts. Note that we are capable of wholesome deeds, which bring positive results. Both the progressive and regressive forces are well known to us. We progress and decline according to which of the 'wolves' we feed by our actions (body, speech, and mind). More accurately, it is the intentions we indulge and the efforts we give to them, that affect our fate. When they are guided by the *dharma*, we have gratifying results. But it is all too easy to slip into *samsaric* patterns that drag us down towards *dukkha*. This second circle is a reminder that a reputation as a 'good' person (perhaps a 'Good Buddhist') counts for little or nothing. We dare not rely on the approval or expectations of other people. A more beneficial approach is to discover the appropriate patterns that improve our present condition as we apply *dharmic* understandings.

Wheel of Life: Inner Circles[203]

Six Realms

In the third circle, we step into a mythic world where six distinct realms exist in parallel universes. From the fiery depths of the inferno to the serene realm of the gods, each realm has its own unique characteristics and inhabitants. Through the six realms, we can discover something of the range of possible existences – each with its pain and danger. But also, we see their cure and comfort in a buddha figure.

The traditional understanding of the six realms assumes a pattern of rebirth in which we are born into this or that condition because of our past actions and attitudes. *Samsara* without a *dharma*-led escape, leads to endless rebirths. Our secular and pragmatic approach emphasises the renewals and reformations that can come by living the Eightfold Path. We can move from one mental state to another. We are not 'stuck' by our past actions. We can change our fate by what we do now.

We will look at each realm, following the traditional pattern as illustrated in the Wheel of Life (Inner Circles) above.

The Realm of the Gods

At the top of this circle is a picture of pleasure. Life is good, with every desire catered to. The gods got to that position by their actions, 'good deeds' which lack the ultimate elements of skilful *karma*: altruism and selflessness. The gods' desires do not include their deepest needs and exclude them from their ultimate contentment.

At the edge of their realm are the branches of a tree that is rooted outside it. This is a symbol of good fortune which has come from others' efforts. The gods benefit from their own efforts, but often from others as well. We place ourselves in the god realm when we dream of holding a winning lottery ticket with wealth beyond all ordinary expectations. It will come to us because of the contributions of people who never had us in mind. Much of the Western success formulae promise great rewards for relatively little effort – tempting to the greedy rooster within us.

Ignorance is present when we focus on *samsara*'s version of unassailable contentment. Some versions of the Wheel counter this by showing the need for protection from assailants, who jealously want in. Others show undiluted bliss. Some meditators (adepts and wannabe adepts) look to pleasurable altered consciousness (the *jhanas*) as their goal. But Gotama never shared that view. Insight, not pleasure, is the highest aim of meditation because it removes the barriers that keep us in *samsara*.

The gods' lives are not trouble-free, however. Those who are jealous of their apparent blessings cause a lot of trouble and demand many counter efforts. In some depictions, this realm includes troops defending their borders from such incursions.

What is the Buddha's message to the gods? He plays a song of Impermanence, reminding them that 'the dream' of a wholly pleasurable life will end. Sometimes our privileges and power are undercut by our foolish decisions or a run of bad luck. Sometimes 'the dream' turns into a nightmare of unfulfillment. And sometimes the means of gaining our 'divine' status harms others, distorting our character and making enemies. Whatever the consequences of our actions, they cannot keep us from the inevitable end to every life.

These gods are not eternal. They share a universal aspect of *dukkha*: their ultimate Impermanence. They, too, will die. They, too, need the *dharma*.

The Realm of the Titans

Going clockwise on the wheel takes us to the Titans or demi-gods, who have immense strength. They do not pursue bliss but power and material gain. They are jealous and hateful, triggered by others' pleasure and treasure. Their characteristic harmfulness is directed at others but also makes them miserable. If only their strength could be directed at helping others, they would be able to help themselves! Some versions of the Wheel show a Titan jealously chopping down the tree that benefits the gods, thus forfeiting the fruit on their side as well.

What can the Buddha do to help the Titans live better lives? He holds the sword of wisdom to cut through their self-harming and destructive, unskilful thinking. They need to see that there is a more effective force than brute strength.

The Animal Realm

Living like an animal, in the Wheel's view, is to live without the perspectives that our minds provide. Animals are in constant danger from themselves and humankind. They are led by sensual instincts (for food and sex), which cannot be fully fulfilled, so they are not content.

> "The scattered animals on the face of the world... small creatures, worms, insects, birds, wild animals, and so forth, each have their particular sufferings of heat, cold, hunger, thirst, being eaten by each other [with] measureless illness and affliction... are tormented by hunters, fishermen, and birds of prey."[204]

Today, of course, we are aware of the suffering that climate change is causing many species. The terror of this realm includes the lack of dignity we suffer when we are pushed by our animal nature to be less than fully human. The Buddha is present with the wisdom sword in his hand, to cut away their ignorance. When we behave as animals we need this radical surgery.

The Hell Realm

Hell, for Buddhists, does not envision eternal punishment. But the state of unremitting pain – physical, emotional, and mental. It can be driven by guilt for past unskilful actions or trauma received in other people's hands. It can reflect severe mental illness, the despair that comes from failed relationships, or assumptions that bar any hope. "Hell is other people" (a line from Jean-Paul Sartre's play, *No Exit*) – and a hundred other sources.

The different versions of the Wheel depict the torments of hell as extreme heat and/or cold. The experiences are symbolised by severe tortures, which we take as symbols of people's inner experiences. How does the Buddha provide a way out of this absorbing state? In some, he holds up a jar of nectar, symbolising generosity. In others, he clears the path to allow escape. Some say his presence represents the virtue of patience and the encouragement that there is another kind of living where people are understanding and compassionate.

The Realm of the Hungry Ghosts

"Hungry Ghosts" are never satisfied with what they have. They are often depicted as having large, distended bellies but tiny mouths which will never be able to ingest sufficient food or drink to meet their desires. We might think of people with any kind of addiction or those with inappropriate ambitions which cannot be met. Their only remedy is to partake of *dharma* nectar. The smallest amount will stretch their mouths to an ever-increasing portion of the deepening satisfactions of *dharma* living.

The Human Realm

To be human is a great advantage. We have a range of experiences that can be moved by a sense of suffering. Yet we can also sense joy and love. Thus, we have the motivation to seek full Awakening and the ability to express our Buddha Nature. With both 'heart' (emotion) and 'head' (rationality), we can contact and realise our true potential and defeat the barriers to realizing it. As Gotama proved, our humanity is such that can recognise and overcome all the impediments to enlightenment by taking all Twelve Steps to our ultimate freedom. With the proper care and nutrients, the seeds of faith within us can keep growing. To be human is a great blessing – the most hopeful realm to dwell in. Humans have a balanced sense of reality. Our *dukkha* will motivate us to seek something more than our present life. Our ability to recognise the dangers within every realm gives us a sense that nothing is truly safe and secure except the *dharma*. The Middle Way is our best hope of escaping *samsara*.

One Thing Leads to Another

The most difficult part of the Wheel of Life to decipher is the outer circle, with its twelve depictions of an unawakened life. This is known as the Twelve *Nidanas* (also called the *Nidana* Chain). *Nidana* is Pali for 'source' or 'origin'.

"The Sanskrit word *nidana* means cause or cause of existence. Shakyamuni is said to have taught the twelve-linked chain of causation in answer to the question of why people have to experience the sufferings of aging and death. Each link in the chain is a cause that leads to the next." Nichiren Buddhism Library.[205]

These twelve illustrations on the outer circle present twelve vivid pictures of causation (dependent origination): 'Because of one thing, another happens'. Each is a state of mind – and each resultant action depends on its predecessor. It is not focused on the consequences of our individual intentional actions (the fruit of our *karma*) so much as the inevitable results of being human.

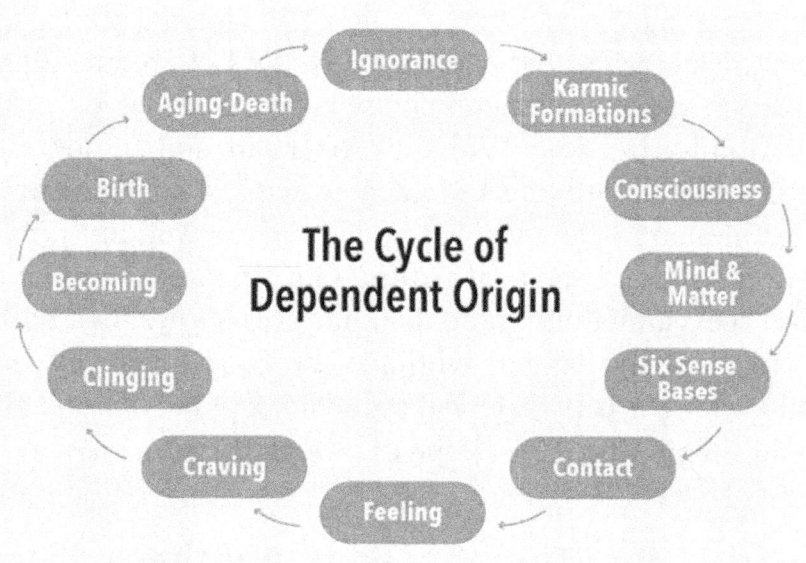

The portrayals of the twelve elements of the chain of life are not uniform. A common explanation is described below.

(1) We begin life with a fundamental **ignorance** of our nature and potential (often pictured as a blind woman).

(2) Then, we explore who we are by doing things. These '*karmic* **formations**' are pictured as a potter throwing pots, discarding the ones that are not working. Thus, we progress by 'trial and error'.

(3) Then our **consciousness** develops, a process Gotama described in the Five Clusters, pictured as a restless monkey.

(4) From this we then gain a sense of self, in terms of 'name and form', **mind and matter**. It is depicted as a boat with two paddlers.

(5) This dualistic self-consciousness leads to further differentiations. We thus fragment the whole with our **six senses**, including the mind, presented as a tent with six windows.

(6) Our senses lead us to **contact** the world, symbolised by a couple making love.

(7) We experience **feelings** (sensations), presented as a man with an arrow in his eye.

(8) This develops within us **craving**, also termed 'thirst', visualised as someone who has stolen fruit from a tree.

(9) Such craving naturally inclines us to **clinging**. A man with his treasure hoard depicts it.

(10) Clinging leads to a recurring desire to become more than we are, designated as **becoming**, symbolised by people swept along by a watery torrent.

(11) This existence promotes and channels an endless and wearisome series of new beginnings, termed **birth**, pictured as a woman bearing a baby.

(12) But, as sure as we're born (reborn), we will experience **aging and death** (without the contentment we have longed for). This is illustrated by a couple hobbling along on their last legs or a body being taken for burial.

A Contemporary Wheel of Life

The Wheel of Life reflects the faith of those living within ancient Asian cultures and their Buddhist worldview.[206] If such a Wheel were created today, no doubt the assumptions of modern psychology, neurology, and perhaps even physics would shape it differently.

Social justice issues are not a concern in the original Wheel. But if produced in our time they no doubt would. To do otherwise would not be seeing 'things as they really are'.

Thus, with tongue firmly in cheek, Derric Drda recommends that we "Form the 'no evil' mudra [hand position] by gently putting your thumbs into your ears and using your fingers to cover your eyes. From within your peaceful bubble, spend as much time as possible not thinking about poverty, war, racism, imperialism, global warming, mass extinction, injustice, inequality, white privilege, destructive nationalism, and other things that would bum you out."[207]

Sadly, this reflects some contemporary practices of meditation and mindfulness. I know Buddhists who boast that they do not look or listen to the news. But a modern *Bodhisattva*, showing compassion for all. (S)he does well to become acquainted with the suffering of her fellow human beings and engage with at least some of the actions and organisations that can meet our common plight.

Drda's book *The Four Global Truths*[208] not only discusses the reality and roots of global suffering, but its relief as well. It is fruitful reading for modern *Bodhisattvas*.

We're Here for Good

Most religions offer an ultimate escape from "the world" into which we've been born to some heavenly alternative. Paradise (no more pain and the ultimate pleasures) is attractive – at least to many billions of people over thousands of years. Although the New Testament contains a vision of "being in the world, not of it", it also speaks of "a new heaven and a new earth" replacing the unacceptable present.[209] A religious Buddhist would affirm rebirth as a way of bettering our presence on this planet (over repeated lifetimes) until one is ready to transcend it all.

Secularists tend to be sceptical or agnostic of that ideal. We replace it with a vision of a pervasive transformation here and now, in this lifetime. We are encouraged that this is what Gotama and thousands of his immediate followers – perhaps millions over the years after him – experienced. They chose to escape the culture and values depicted in the Wheel and follow the clues to achieving transcendent living.

Every detail in the Wheel of Life is meant to create a hunger for liberation. Whether we see our future births in terms of successive lifetimes or simply fresh starts, we need the Buddha and his *dharma* for a more skilful approach to living. The alternative is being stuck in the endless rounds of *samsara*.

The Wheel is confronting us with our bondage and shouting to us, 'Strive to Awaken!'

Over to You!

1. Can you experience the Wheel of Life as a mirror to understanding some aspects of your past and present life?

2. Does the Realm of the Gods attract you, or can you see why it, too, needs to be escaped?

3. Is there any particular aspect of the Wheel of Life which speaks deeply to you about yourself? About another person?

Reflection: Beautiful and Brief

"Veneration of the Three Jewels"[210]

17.
Spiritual, Religious, or Both?

"I'm a Buddhist, I'm a Muslim, I'm a Christian. It all comes down to the same thing. You're either in a loving place or an unloving loving place."
Jim Carrey[211]

"All religions are sustained by the same circular, impenetrable logic that transcends probability…"
Carlos Alba[212]

"Buddhist teachings are not a religion; they are a science of mind."
Jack Kornfield[213]

"The religion of the future will be a cosmic religion. It should transcend a personal God and avoid dogmas and theology. Covering both the natural and the spiritual, it should be based on a religious sense arising from the experience of all things, natural and spiritual, as a meaningful unity. Buddhism answers this description."
Attributed to Albert Einstein[214]

"I'm Spiritual but Not Religious"

I've heard it a thousand times. I've said it myself, first as a humanist, then with a Christian identification, and now as a Buddhist. But what is "spiritual"? What is "religious"? There is no clear-cut differentiation between spirituality and religion. Both seek (or give) answers to some of life's deepest questions:

- What is the ultimate meaning of life?
- What is my ultimate purpose?
- What values should I hold, and why?
- Do things happen for a reason?
- Is there a greater/higher power than humanity? If so, what is its nature, and how do we relate to it?
- What are my connections with others?
- What happens when we die?
- Is there life after death? If so, what is its nature?
- How can I know such unseen things?
- What can be said in the face of unanswerable questions?
- How should I face personal, social, and ecological crises?
- How can I have certainty and hope?

Broadly speaking, the difference between spirituality and religion is not so much in the questions we ask as to how they are answered. Spirituality tends to welcome individual and independent judgment, while religion is more oriented to communal affirmation under the authority of its teachers and traditions.

Neither identification determines whether a person will be kind and compassionate, humble and respectful of other people, determined to grow in understanding and practice, and devoted to the wellbeing of others. I have known sceptics and fundamentalists, whose views differ vastly from my own spiritual beliefs, who seem to me to be stellar examples of humanity. And yet, I sometimes find it hard to affirm the wholesomeness of some people with whom I might agree on almost every articulated view. The personality and character of an individual is more important than their label.

How We Do Community is Crucial

We have alluded to the importance of community (*sangha*) in Chapter Fourteen. I want to emphasise its significance for religion and spirituality. It is our source of inspiration and support, as my *sangha* affirms every week, and I acknowledge every day. How we engage with this communal aspect sets the tone of our experience.

If our community demands agreement with its declared views and subservience to its leaders, as the most constraining and constrictive organisations can do, the oxygen of free inquiry and critical questioning will be noticeable by its absence. For some the security of believing a final truth has been discovered provides a welcome comfort, stability and assurance. But their peace of mind can be shattered when the leadership changes its mind. My son's Amish community (strongly believing that the old ways are best and should not be dishonoured) violated a cardinal principle of non-involvement with worldly politics. The Bishop declared that everyone should vote for Donald Trump, as God's preferred candidate. Dissenters risked excommunication (exclusion from the community) and subsequent 'shunning'. Impermanence and dynamic change are evidenced, for good or ill, in everything.

All the communities I frequent, whether identifying as secular or spiritual, encourage their members to think for themselves and to discuss points of view with due consideration for different interpretations. By doing so they provide a welcoming home base for those who would not relish groups which operate with more rigid and inflexible understandings. At its best this more 'liberal' spirituality provides the security of respect for every member and recognition of our journey as legitimate and wholesome. This is the nourishment that I need to sustain my individual journey, and it seems that other pragmatic and secular Buddhists do too.

Inevitable Ambiguities

Gotama understood that what we experience as "reality" reflects a significant amount of subjectivity and objective limitations. He described how our consciousness comes through a process (*skhanda* analysis) which cannot be wholly subjective. As well, our bodies receive limited data from our senses and our brains. When we realise that our conscious perceptions and opinions come from our processing of sense data by our neurological system, we can see that our experience of 'reality' is limited and somewhat skewed. Consider our vision as an example:

> "Of all the possible photon wavelengths out there, our cone cells detect but a small sliver, typically in the range of about 380 to 720 nanometres – what we call the visible spectrum. Below our narrow perceptual band is the infrared and radio spectrum, with the latter's longer, less energetic wavelengths ranging from a millimetre to kilometres in length."[215]

All our senses have an inability to register the totality of the reality we are living with. We can only hear within a specific range of frequencies. Our sense of touch is constrained by the density and sensitivity of our nerve endings, which vary in different parts of the body and are unable to register everything they encounter. Our taste and smell are limited by the number of taste buds and olfactory receptors we possess. Of course, individual people have their own limitations, such as the disappearance of taste that some covid 19 sufferers have experienced and the hearing loss that many of us wrestle with.

The human brain, our species' greatest asset with its mind-boggling capabilities, also comes with limitations. Our confidence in its veracity is similarly undercut. As Dr. Jim Taylor puts it,

> "Perception acts as a lens through which we view reality. Our perceptions influence how we focus on, process, remember, interpret, understand, synthesize, decide about, and act on reality. In doing so, our tendency is to assume that how we perceive reality is an accurate representation of what reality truly is. But it's not."[216]

Gotama's approach to "things as they really are" is not referring to an accurate perception of what our senses convey to our brains, but rather a way of living without any unnecessary suffering in a way that is truly wholesome and helpful. He did not pronounce on the physics or metaphysics of what we encounter.

If this lack of ultimate 'truth' relates to the material world, how much more so to our concepts, which are shaped by our conditioning and our personal preferences. The belief in infallible revelations may be comfortable and reassuring, but it cannot be justified. The irrefutable ambiguities and limitations of our perceptions means that all speculations concerning spiritual (unverifiable) realities must remain tentative. Our sense of meaning and our values are similarly subjective. But this does not mean they are invalid. Such spiritual understanding shape our ability to journey through life with purposefulness, inner peace, and skilfulness.

A pragmatic spirituality reflects on our convictions concerning how to live and why, with a resulting practice that shapes our lives. Our pragmatic faith will evaluate concepts and convictions, such kindness and compassion for all beings, rebirth, Buddha Nature and inter-being by asking about their outcome: Is it leading me into increased contentment and decreased suffering? If so, why should we abandon them. If not, it would be wise to reconsider their worth.

Toxic and Wholesome Behaviours

It is easy to condemn religion for its faults. But it is important to recognise its positive effects as well. While it is true that history exposes the scandals, cruel and corrupting religious crusades, jihads, pogroms genocides, and support for ethnic cleansing. The sexual and other abuses perpetrated by a minority of religious leaders are becoming increasingly clear, alienating many from their former faith. But we cannot dismiss religion as a whole because of these horrors. The influence of religion upon sacrificial service and inspiring accomplishments counterbalances and can outweigh the negatives.

As well, we can recognise that Atheists are not exempt from colossal harm, as we see in the brutal history of nations led by Joseph Stalin (The Soviet Union), Mao Zedong (China), Pot Pol (Cambodia), and Kim Il-sung (North Korea). Destructive behaviours by individuals in their homes and communities in any nation adds immeasurably to human suffering.

The dark side of human nature, whether religious or not, is at the root of this colossal suffering. But there are countless examples of the best in humanity, which religious organisations seek to nurture. The inherent possibilities of a wholesome life are expressed in Buddha Nature, Christ Nature, and Fitah, the Muslim equivalent. Other faiths have similar concepts.

People from all religions (as well their nonreligious counterparts) have been inspirational for their loving, generous and sometimes sacrificial efforts. This includes direct service as well as financial giving.

A great deal of money is raised for a variety of good causes in churches, mosques and temples. A Civil Society study in 2024 reports that British Muslims average giving totalled £708 over 12 months. Committed Christians contributed £314 a month to good causes, almost five times the UK monthly giving average.

The Stewardship organisation stresses that "stewardship isn't just about money" and list different ways people have been serving the needs of others by "using our gifts wisely, serving others humbly, making time for what matters, embracing sacrifice, and caring for creation."[217] The websites of religious charities detail the variety of projects they support, which includes the 'sweat equity' of volunteers.[218]

For all the bad press religion attracts there are many more 'good news' stories to report.

Advantages of Religion: An Example

Besides meeting basic human needs, religious people have made significant contributions to society, as well as providing individuals with spiritual resources, such as a sense of transcendence, community, meaning, and values. Much charity work, promotion of universal human dignity, and social reconstruction is linked to churches, mosques, temples and *sanghas*.

An excellent example of the outward and inward benefits of religion, is the "new vehicle" (*Navayana*) of the "Ambedkar Movement" in India. It was established among the former 'untouchables', now known as Dalits – still at the bottom of the Hindu caste system[219] (the legitimacy of which Buddhists deny). Dr. B. R. Ambedkar was a Dalit who progressed to earn a law degree and two doctorates, becoming the first Indian national to gain a PhD. He dedicated his life to the liberation of his fellow untouchables. They have been victimised in a most exploitative and brutal, dehumanising way for many centuries. Millions have been liberated to a dignified and fulfilling life through this movement.

Dr. Ambedkar was not naturally religious and considered leading his people into Marxism.[220] He chose the slogan "Liberty, Equality, and Fraternity" from the anti-religious French Revolution. But he became convinced that something more than a secular political movement was needed to empower his people and counter their dehumanisation, namely a sense of transcendence that could revolutionise action.

Considering the available religious options, Dr. Ambedkar eliminated theistic options such as Christianity and Islam as illusionary and socially conservative. He judged Marxism and Buddhism the two most likely ideologies to empower his fellow Dalits to gain self-respect, confidence, and the endurance to participate in the ongoing social liberation. After carefully evaluating the advantages of the two, he decided that Buddhism was best positioned to be the agent of transformation because of its inward emphasis and its founder's implicit rejection of class divisions.

At a rally, pictured below, he personally led half a million ex-untouchables into Buddhism. Ambedkar's version of Buddhism was established in a book, *The Buddha and His Dharma* - published after his untimely death in December 1956. His perspective was spiritual, social, and political. Ambedkar-inspired movements are still going strong in India.

Dr. Ambedkar's Address to ex-untouchable Indians
October 14, 1956, at Deekshabhoomi in Nagpur

The Ambedkar movement is an example of the power of interpreting "Buddhism" to suit the deepest and most pressing needs of a people.

> "In evaluating Ambedkar's Buddhism, it is useful to remember that radical reinterpretations of the Buddha's message have often been presented as its true or original teaching. Contemporary scholars have argued that Buddhist hermeneutics, the study of variant readings of the Buddha's teaching and the discovery of new meanings and interpretations, has been going on ever since Shakyamuni held up a flower and smiled in silence."[221]

Transcendence

What empowers all the acts of kindness and compassion? Is it doctrine? Inspiring examples? A supernatural or suprapersonal force? We cannot say for sure. But those who affirm that the realities we experience includes a spiritual dimension testify to experiencing some kind of power or presence which seems both larger (perhaps infinitely greater) than their individuality.

Most religions emphasise that their God (or equivalent) is "transcendent" – above and beyond humanity and the natural order. This divine being can directly and intentionally influence our lives and transform our dysfunction so that we, too, can transcend the world. The Buddhist concept of transcendence is quite different. Through the transforming *dharma*, we can overcome our present, poisoned self and thus develop a more appropriate relationship with the world.

Transcendence comes from the Latin prefix *trans-*, meaning 'beyond' and the word *scandare*, meaning 'to climb.' When you achieve transcendence, you have gone beyond ordinary human limitations.[222] But what limitations do we go beyond? For Buddhists it is our instinctive reactivity (greed, hatred, and delusion).

The prospect of transcending our own reactivity is at the heart of the good news of Gotama's Four Realities. This does not mean our lives will be free from unavoidable pains and stress (what Buddhists came to call *dukkha dukkha*). But, when we experience pain and other unpleasant realities, we can respond appropriately, rather than react unskilfully.

Do Buddhists Pray and Worship?

One of the central religious practices is prayer, often as though addressing a God or deity to ask favours for oneself (intercession) or simply to express devotion and faith. Many assume that since Buddhists do not affirm a creating, intervening, judging God, they could not possibly pray. But there is a real sense in which Buddhist expressions of good wishes for others reflect a secular form of prayer. In religious homes, meals are often marked by table graces. A Buddhist equivalent recognises the bounty of the earth and the many people who were instrumental in its delivery to us. I was introduced to this thanksgiving custom at events sponsored by Amida Buddhism and The Western Chan Fellowship. One that I love is: "This food represents the joys and suffering of many. May we be strengthened by it, and with that strength contribute to the good of others."[223]

An established practice in most Buddhist traditions is to "venerate the Buddha": honouring his excellence, recognising his worth, and showing gratitude for his example and teaching. This religious behaviour need not imply "divine worship". Yet, many Buddhists have a sense of Gotama as a Supreme and Eternal Presence (similar to God).

When leading a weekly ceremony for asylum seekers at the Dungaval Immigration Removal Centre. I saw many relate to the Buddha as a divine figure with the inclination and ability to bestow favours in a direct way.

Gotama never taught the existence or benefit of such a figure. Within contemporary Buddhism I see a clear and present danger of reflecting a 'theistic tendency'. In his discussion of "Why I gave up finding my religion", John Horgan shares his 'regretful' conclusion that,

> "Buddhism is functionally theistic, even if it avoids the "G" word. …[It] espouses reincarnation, which holds that after death our souls are re-instantiated in new bodies, and

karma, the law of moral cause and effect. Together, these tenets imply the existence of some cosmic judge who, like Santa Claus, tallies up our naughtiness and niceness before rewarding us with rebirth as a cockroach or as a saintly lama [Tibetan monk]."[224]

Thankfully, we need not give up all the positive aspects of Gotama's faith to abandon supernaturalist interpretations of his thought. Our Buddhist life can remain vital if we allow our interpretation of it to mature with our changing understandings. To do otherwise is like a Christian who refuses to alter the faith he formed at Sunday School.

Deep Agnosticism

Perhaps it was agnosticism that led the Buddha to stay silent on topics that his contemporaries loved to discuss. But another reason for his silence was when the topic was irrelevant to Awakening.

Stephen Batchelor speculates on how a modern agnostic Buddhism might express itself.[225] He would remain silent about issues that rely on supernatural or paranormal 'knowledge'. Agnostic Buddhists would neither proffer nor seek 'metaphysical' answers for "consolation". But it would provide a very positive programme for Awakening in this one life (the only one we can be certain about).

Agnosticism is "derived from the Greek *agnōstos* (unknowable). Thomas Huxley coined the term in 1869. Agnostics recognise that no one can know of the existence of anything beyond the phenomena of their experience."[226]

Stephen Batchelor uses the term "deep agnosticism" as a rigorous and thorough focus on applying Gotama's principles for skilful living, supplemented by an emphasis on the imagination. Batchelor is convinced that the arts are a key to contemporary *dharma* living. Rather than trying to understand what lies beyond our abilities to know, we seek the depth of expressing what is often hidden in our subconscious. It is there that the barriers to, and the empowerment for, our deepest flourishing lie.

Spiritual, Secular, and Religious

Religion can provide a rich source of community, culture, and personal meaning for many people. It offers moral and ethical guidelines, a sense of belonging, and often helps individuals find comfort in times of difficulty. Dismissing religion entirely might overlook these positive aspects and the profound impact it has had on human history and individual lives.

It's also worth considering the diverse ways in which people experience and practice their faith. Some find spiritual fulfilment through rituals and traditions, while others may draw inspiration from the teachings and philosophies within their religion.

There can be much to embrace and celebrate in religion, so it might be foolish to dismiss it. I still say, in some conversations, that "I am spiritual, not religious". When I do, I am aware of my own tendency to accept certain aspects of religion - each received as a helpful thought or practice – and to reject others. When religion serves to slow or even block spiritual growth, I recognise that they are no longer contributing in a positive way. Sometimes, when asked, I'll say, "Spiritual and religious, and secular!" For me, the first is by far the most important. How about you?

Over to You!

1. Looking at the list of questions that start this chapter, which are the most important ones for you?

2. Ideally (for you) how might a community best explore the deepest and most pressing questions in your life?

3. What are your attitudes towards religion?

A Secular Buddhist Spirituality

Reflection: Time to Fly

One of the earliest seated Buddha Icons[227]

Postlude

"There is one thing about *dharma* that I am entirely sure of: It is for people. The Buddha's teachings are not a cold philosophy designed merely to rearrange the concepts in our minds. They are a living act of compassion intended to show us how to open our hearts."
Hsing Yun, Chinese Adept, Lotus in a Stream[228]

"If you meet the Buddha on the road, kill him!"
Linyi Yixuan (Ninth-century Chinese Buddhist monk)

What Now?

Where is Gotama's *dharma* leading you? If the teaching were limited to ethics, it would provide principles for our actions and relationships. If it were essentially a philosophy, it could orient us to its wisdom. As a way of life, it would show us how to live well. But in all these, we would still have to decide on the relevance and consequences for ourselves and others. The *dharma* confronts us and demands a response. But it does not and cannot tell us what is appropriate for our circumstances. We must exercise our best judgment.

Linyi Yixuan's provocative suggestion that 'if we meet the Buddha on our journey, we should kill him' is meant to shake us out of our expectations of what Awakening will be for us. If we conceptualise Awakening only in terms of an idealised model (Gotama, for instance), we will inevitably limit its unique possibilities for us. All Buddhas share much in common, but their authentic realisations are not identikit clones. As conditioned beings, interacting with an innumerable number of influences, each Buddha has a distinctive form. This will be true of every Awakening.

Finding Our Own Path

Buddhism, understood as living the *dharma*, includes a confident programme for gaining a radically new sense of our own dynamics. It is often more fluid than we might imagine. The *dharma* is not a set of specific, inviolable directions, but guidelines for our own discovery. The multidimensional potential which Awakening represents will likely exceed our expectations and calculations.

For Buddhists Awakening comes by following Gotama's recommended path and expressing our Buddha Nature, which we trust is loving, wise, creative, adequate for the moment and relevant to the conditions we face. The process is developmental taking us from set concepts to an intuitive and spontaneous experience. It helps us be mindful and aware of ourselves and our surroundings, including a consciousness of the multiple factors influencing our thoughts and actions. While the process might seem solid, the awakened life is dynamic and needs to be reborn as our circumstances change.

Each of us will understand the central message of the *dharma* according to our own experience. Some might focus on the release of all unnecessary pain and dissatisfaction. Others may notice on our new ability to overcome our reactive nature (greed, hatred, delusion). Still others could see it in terms of discovering or acquiring the ability to live according to the Eightfold Path, Twelve Steps, or Four

Tasks. What the Buddha wanted us to experience cannot be limited to a particular emphasis nor a single pattern of implementation. His words are helpful, but we must go beyond them to apply them. Thus, we awaken to an experience of life so free and so different that he called it "the Other Shore".

Be Prepared to Change

Buddhism offers so many riches in so many different contexts that you can stay within its immense tent with its variety of understandings and practices. You never need to be stagnant, bored, or without challenges for further growth.

Does this mean we must keep switching our chosen *sangha*? I've learned that that is unnecessary. Awakening and being open to fresh thinking does not necessarily mean shifting your social context. Sometimes, relationships do need to be terminated. But many people find a better alternative by working through their problems and implementing a partnership that can contain, even honour, profound differences. This is called a 'large tent' or a 'broad Church' in politics. It is expressed as a mutually enriching tolerance.

Part of our inbuilt reactivity is to cherish the familiar and thus resist change. We become attached to yesterycar's patterns, rejecting all that contradicts them. In Christian circles, it is often said that maturing adults need to go beyond the simplistic understandings of Sunday School teaching. The same essential point applies to those embracing Buddhism. Our initial *dharma*-based insights need to mature as we reflect on how to walk the Path to Awakening. We dare not become too comfortable with our *dharma* understanding and practice if it keeps us from moving forward to Awakening. As the saying goes, there are times when the *dharma* comforts our distress and others when it challenges our comforts.

The most arduous shifts can be those of emphasis. We can restrict our practice to a few aspects of the Buddha's Eight Paths and Twelve Steps. We can become too comfortable with limited favourite patterns and ignore the variety recommended by Gotama and the challenging patterns that have developed since his time.

Others might sense it and react adversely when we change from established norms. Warm relationships may cool, and questions may be raised. We might feel disconnected and unsupported and fear that our authentic self-expression is no longer welcome, even with our attempts to be diplomatic and irenic. We might sense that a different community will be more understanding and accepting. There are times when we need to move on. Such a radical action may be appropriate. However, it could be an unnecessary evasion of the complex and fearful work of being an authentic individual within a community. As the 'shadow work' specialist Nancy Levin stresses that we can hide who we are from ourselves as we seek to hide ourselves from others.[229]

A personal example may provide clarity. Over the past decade, I have seen how my desire for the security of spiritual, intellectual, and social stability has led me to seek and adopt different Christian and Buddhist traditions as wholly reliable and unproblematic. But after about five years, I become disillusioned with the actual realities of the church or *sangha* I settled with – and would latch on to another promising tradition and expect it to be an ideal experience. But the fact is that human nature, in its complex imperfections, easily compromises high ideals. A mature approach is to recognise that fact and work within it – beginning with oneself, not 'them'. Only occasionally, or never, will we need to embrace a radically new social context. I've learned that it's OK to stay within a familiar setting and concentrate on making radical changes within ourselves. I need not leave a community to move on from its consensus. And there will likely be some appropriate spiritual friends within its membership.

Now that I am living in the final quartile of life, I see with increased clarity the meaning behind the saying, "To everything, there is a season and a purpose under heaven."[230] As we face different stages in our lives, we change our priorities and patterns. Sometimes, the Pete Seeger song, *Turn, Turn, Turn*, surfaces in my mind, repeating over and over the turn, turn, turn off the changes I am experiencing. It reminds me of the need to assess and evaluate my life, with readjustments as needed. The Buddha who shared his *dharma* treasures is no fundamentalist dictator, demanding a static, uniform response. Rather, Gotama would encourage us to determine what is credible and appropriate for our specific situations.

A Parable of Self-discovery

The Reverend Russell Conwell was a New England Baptist preacher and popular speaker. During a visit to archaeological sites in Persia in 1870, his guide told him a story. Conwell retold it in a lengthy book published in 1890. But it became known worldwide as a speech he delivered 6,152 times: "Acres of Diamonds". The following is a summary.

Al-Afed was a Persian farmer whose orchards, gardens, and fields of grain made him a very rich man. He was content and grateful for his lot, which included a wonderful family. But his life was undermined by a visiting Buddhist monk, the villain of the story. The Monk spoke of diamonds, which he described as congealed sunlight. These gems could make a man as rich as Croesus.

Though the farmer was satisfied and well-to-do, he became poor in spirit through a desire for treasure beyond imagining. This led him to sell his farm, leave his family, and travel great distances to search for precious stones. But he never found any. Sick at heart after many years of fruitless searching, Al-Afed died by throwing himself into the sea near Barcelona.

Later, the same Buddhist Monk revisited the farm, which was now under new ownership. He noticed a rock the young farmer had discovered in his garden and placed it on his parlour mantle. "You have a great treasure there", exclaimed the monk. "No, I found a pretty rock in my garden." Hearing this ignorant reply, the Monk explained it was a diamond and that diamonds were one of Earth's greatest treasures. He led the farmer back into the garden area. The new farm owner discovered acres of diamonds in their backyard.

Conwell's original story had an isolationist perspective: 'Why seek your fortune in distant lands when America has all the resources anyone needs to prosper?' That is not the moral I'm recommending from this story! A more helpful point is that we have diamond-like minds, which can lead us to discover all we need for true prosperity and flourishing. The first Buddhist monk, Gotama, helps us realise the same.

Go For It!

My hope for this book is that it will encourage many to reach their fullest potential: the human ideal exemplified in the life and teaching of Siddhartha Gotama. I have worked hard to present a tantalising, seductive smorgasbord for you to consider and apply for your own good and the good of others. But you'll be the judge of that!

Perhaps you will have a sense that the *dharma* is deeply familiar and an authentic help. You can explore and apply Gotama's teaching, in whole or in part, to see how it might work in your life. Those already familiar with the *dharma* can test whether a secular Buddhism can inform or expand their spiritual understanding and contribute to their well-being.

All the different approaches contained in traditional and untraditional Buddhism are 'appropriate' if they contribute to our spiritual growth and human flourishing. Although the many available Buddhist understandings contain some major differences, they tend to agree that the ultimate goal is Awakening (*bodhi*), contentment (*sukha*), freedom (*moksha*), and *nirvana* (liberation from greed, hatred and delusion).

What matters most is to discover what resonates within your whole being and contributes to your skilfulness. For this to happen, it is essential that you know yourself as you are, and you are willing to change in order to grow and then grow some more. Some may sense a need for a religious Buddhism. Others will favour a secular approach. Many will want a mix of both. Whatever way you choose to do so, you can heed the Four Realities and learn to walk the transformative Eightfold Path.

It is helpful – I might say necessary, to be aware of both our Buddha Nature (our positive potential) and our Mara Nature (the dark side of human possibility). Once we have opened our eyes to them, we can access the gentle *dharmic* reality within and beyond our individuality.

All this is doable. The Eightfold Path and all the Perfections are within our grasp. We can draw from the available wisdom we've discussed in this book (and beyond!) to meet our challenges with positive results.

What is the Buddhist hope, with its implicit promise of vitality and contentment? The short answer is the awakened life. Will you make it your goal to find your personal Awakening? If so, how might you seek it? Your answer to this question will determine whether and how you apply the *dharma* to your life.

Now, as it has ever been, it is… **Over to You!**

A SECULAR BUDDHIST SPIRITUALITY

Reflection: A Never-Ending Journey

Teaching his five ascetic friends[231]

Appendix: The First Turning of the *Dharma* Wheel, Paraphrased

Introduction

"The First Turning of the *Dharma* Wheel" discourse (the *Dhammacakkappavattana Sutta*), often called "The Deer Park Sermon" is framed as Gotama's uninterrupted talk to the five ascetics he had previously led in an extreme regime of bodily denial.

Soon after his Awakening, he had asked himself, 'Who could understand the complex and subtle thoughts that lead to Awakening?' He thought of the ascetics he had led, and the deer park where they had all enjoyed many times, with many other itinerant spiritual seekers. It is said that he walked the 250 miles (400 kilometres) to the park and enthusiastically shared what led to his liberating experience. This was Gotama's first attempt to summarise his new insights. The message was likely delivered many times after that, becoming a carefully crafted presentation of his *dharma*.

We can imagine that many monks contributed their memories of Gotama's foundational teaching to this discourse and hence it is not a strict historical record.

There are many excellent translations of this key discourse on online sites such as Access to Insight, BuddhaNet, and Sutta Central. My paraphrase, below, is a retelling that explains some concepts that were implicit but unstated in the original. It is worth reading one or more of these translations, either before or after reading my paraphrase, to see what meaning you can draw from this fabulous *sutta*.

The last paragraph reflects a supernaturalism that is out of step with the rest of the *sutta*; It must have been added on sometimes before these key insights were written down (at least 300-400 years after Gotama's death). Some translators leave the passage out because it is so obviously different from the main text.

The Discourse

I, Ananda, am telling you what I heard from Gotama himself. He told me all his teachings, right from the beginning. On one occasion, he was in the deer park at Benares, where the seekers and seers gathered. There, he addressed the five wandering ascetics he had previously led:

"Friends, I have discovered that there are two extremes to avoid when we leave our homes to search for life's meaning. The first extreme is to indulge ourselves in sensual pleasure. Such a life is low, demeaning, vulgar and a diversion from what we are seeking. The second is the opposite approach, abusing the body, which destroys our health and thus impedes our quest. As you know, I have experienced both extremes. But I have discovered a better way to avoid both, which and lead to my Awakening. I call it the Middle Way.

"This Middle Way gave me all we have been seeking: a vision and knowledge of existence as it really is, leading to the peace we all long for and freedom from the reactivity that so often misleads us.

"What is this Middle Way exactly? It is an Eightfold Path, namely,

- appropriate perspective,
- appropriate resolve,
- appropriate speech,
- appropriate action,
- appropriate vocation,
- appropriate effort,
- appropriate mindfulness, and
- appropriate concentration.

"My transformation has come with the discovery of four great realities. Knowing them 'as they really are' is ennobling. It allows us to express the very best in ourselves.

"The first is **the reality of suffering** (pain, stress, and dissatisfaction). From birth, we experience it. We feel it deeply when we age. We know it in sickness, sorrow, and death. It is experienced when we lose the people and the things we love, and when we are drawn to what is loathsome and shameful. Everything we crave and cling to with our five senses will eventually lead to suffering.

"A second ennobling reality concerns **the cause of our unnecessary pain**. It comes from our trying to perpetuate the pleasures of the senses, clinging to them and denying their transitory nature. After a pleasant experience, we deeply desire to continue it forever. But this is impossible! Everything moves on and changes. Trying to get the past back adds to our suffering. Our craving goes a step further.

When things are going well, we want to remain just as we are. When life is miserable, we want our life to end. We simply can't face life as it is: an ever-changing stream of pleasure and discomfort.

"The third and fourth realities are a bright light providing hope of a better way.

"The third is that **our lives do not have to be marked by any self-generated pain**. If the cause lies in us, then the cure does too! Our craving and other unwholesome responses can fade if we give them up, let go of false expectations, and reject our fruitless attempts to deny the changing nature of our experience. But how can this happen?

"The fourth reality tells us **how to gain freedom from this suffering and its causes – the Eightfold Path**. "This path is the way to stop all unnecessary suffering.

"I am sharing with you the insight that came with my Awakening. It came as an intuition, a vision, an understanding that I'd never had before. It happened as I considered my own thoughts and behaviours and those of others.

"What a vision! I grasped the suffering we experience (the First Reality). I saw how it touched my life; that was the First Task.

"In my vision, I saw that we bring this suffering upon ourselves repeatedly (the Second Reality). I understood how this applied to me as much as to anyone; the Second Task.

"My vision did not stop there! I realised that this kind of suffering could cease and that I could be free from it (the

Third Reality). Thus, I experienced a foretaste of the end of my suffering; the Third Task.

"This knowledge is necessary for liberation, but it is insufficient. We need to train and apply ourselves in wholesome living (the Fourth Reality) by learning to walk an Eightfold Path; the Fourth Task

Full Awakening is the fruit of these **four tasks**: To be liberated, each of us must first **comprehend our stress** (our discontent). Then we must **understand its cause** which so often is found within ourselves. Third, we must **verify in our own lives** that it can end. And finally, we must **develop the eightfold practice** that leads to cessation of our suffering. This is the fourth and final task.

"My vision and insight went further. It made the way to end our suffering very clear. I realised that each of the four ennobling realities must be understood, then tested, and finally, they need to be lived consistently. I had to respond to these ennobling realities not by hearsay, but with my own direct experience. And so must you, if you are to Awaken.

"There are three phases for responding to the realities if they are to ennoble us. We must first **understand it**, then **try it out**, and third **embed it** in our lives. If we do these three for each of the four noble truths, we are liberated.

"This was my experience, and I rejoice in it. It can be yours as well.

"Until I understood the necessity of each of these Twelve Steps – applying all three phases to each of the four realities – I could not claim to have discovered a full, supreme Awakening. But when I experienced how things really are, in all Twelve Steps, I could claim to have discovered a full, supreme Awakening. Then I knew that my heart's deliverance was unassailable. I said to myself, 'This is the last birth. Now there is no renewal of being'.

"I could not claim to be fully awake until I had grasped these Twelve Steps fully. My final vision was preceded by much reflection. Had I just pretended to be Awake, it would not have been credible to spiritual seekers, established priests, nor to the forces of good and evil. But once the final, purified and perfected vision came, I could claim to all beings (men and gods, princes and householders, devils and divinities, spiritual seekers and priests), that 'My deliverance can withstand any contrary claim. My Awakening is the best. I now see reality. My heart has been delivered from its burdens and will remain so. I need to seek no further transformation'."

The five wanderers rejoiced when they heard his message. They were all convinced by it.

Kondanna, who was one of the five, was the first to comprehend the *dharma*. During Gotama's talk he exclaimed, "All that is subject to arising is subject to ceasing." This concurred with the Buddha's vision. The wheel of true insight was rolling on! Gotama responded, "Kondanna knows! Kondanna knows!" This explains how he came to be known as Anna-Kondanna (Kondanna Who Knows).

The Gods Rejoice

After the Buddha's discourse, one of the earth gods cried out, "At Benares, in the Deer Park at Isipatana, the matchless wheel of truth has been set rolling by the Blessed One. It will not be stopped by men or gods, not by any positive or negative power nor anyone in the world." Hearing this, all the gods in the six paradises cried out with the same sentiment. This reached the Associates of High Divinity in the realm of pure form. Then, all the gods, in turn, took up the cry. The universe rocked with the sound, and a great light, measureless in its brilliance, shone in the world.

Author's note: This last paragraph, so different from the rest of the sutta, was most likely added by a pious monk at some point in its oral transmission. I include it so that you can be acquainted with the whole of the Discourse as it has come down to us. My personal choice is to ignore it when considering Gotama's dharma.

About the Author

Dennis at his Ordination

Raised in a humanist household, Dr Dennis Oliver (Seng Ting) has promoted human welfare through his work and voluntary service in religious and community development organisations.

Dennis has explored and shared principles of spiritual living in a variety of Christian and Buddhist contexts. He earned the Dr. Missiology from Fuller Theological Seminary, pastored three Canadian congregations and served as a teacher, consultant and lay educator focusing on congregational dynamics. He has worked with a variety of social entrepreneurs and social service organisations in Canada and the UK.

Dennis embraced Buddhism in 1990. He was part-time Buddhist Chaplain at HMP Kilmarnock for ten years. In 2017 he co-founded the Centre for Pragmatic Buddhism in Scotland, which he still serves. He is an ordained Senior Monk (Sensei) with the Order of Pragmatic Buddhism. Dennis authored curricula for community-based organisations, including "Coach Up!" and "Rainbow Thinking Skills".

He has written for a variety of periodicals and books, including **The I Can Attitude**, (Wood Lake Books, 1992) of which John Congram wrote, "In an age of depression and confusion, Dennis Oliver offers hope and a way forward through the stories of ordinary people."

Dennis published **Illustrated Poems and Songs** which reflects his presence in Glasgow's amateur performance circles. This included an evening presentation of Leonard Cohen's songs and a play about the Underground Railway, performed at St. Mungo's Museum. He wrote and produced a one man show with Norman McCallum: "The Buddha Pays a Visit", which was performed twice in Stirling by Mr. McCallum.

Dennis is the father of four and grandfather of five. He lives in Glasgow, Scotland, with his wife Elizabeth and their dog Bryn.

A Secular Buddhist Spirituality

Rebalance Your Life for Contentment and Attainment

Dr. Dennis Oliver presents a broad framework for evaluating the many activities of our lives and envisioning fulfilling goals for a better future. This practical resource helps you determine the kind of life you are seeking, clarify realistic goals for the coming year, and determine reliable approach to achieve them. It does not seek a perfect life (impossible!), but a series of improvements, month by month, based on a reflective assessment of your values and purpose.

Rebalancing Your Life for Contentment and Attainment can help you fashion a realistic approach to future-building that suits your personality and lifestyle. You will be encouraged by listing the positive habits and routines in your life, and by your ability to strengthen them and add new ones. By setting just three to five key goals for the year ahead, you will strengthen your achievement muscles and experience significant change.

It will be published in 2026/27.

CONTENTMENT HERE AND NOW

Notes and References

[1] https://libquotes.com/

[2] Stone Head in Tree Roots. Wat Mahathat, Ayutthaya, Thailand, 14th Century, CE - Photo by Gary Lee Todd; under Creative Commons Licence 3.0

[3] See https://www.thebuddhistsociety.org/page/scriptures-texts and https://www.learnreligions.com/the-pali-canon-450130

[4] "Effectiveness is doing 'the right' things, for example setting right targets to achieve an overall goal (the effect)." "Efficacy is getting things done. It is the ability to produce a desired amount of the desired effect, or success in achieving a given goal." (Quoting from "Efficacy, Effectiveness and Efficiency in the Health Care: The Need for an Agreement to Clarify its Meaning", ©2020 by the authors in their open access article).

[5] https://lbu.edu.np/research/ethical-pragmatic-nature-of-buddhism-conceptual-analysis/

[6] https://www.snsociety.org/

[7] https://secularbuddhistnetwork.org/

[8] https://www.middlewaysociety.org/

[9] https://www.buddhanet.net/e-learning/buddhistworld/mapbud/ By permission of Buddhanet.

[10] The `Mona Lisa Buddha' Dunhuang Museum, China, 5th Century CE Photo by David Stanley Creative Commons License 2.0

[11] "Advice to the Kalamas" (*Kalama Sutta*)

[12] For example, George E. Vaillant: *Spiritual Evolution, A Scientific Defence of Faith* (2008, Broadway Books) and Ken Wilbur: *The Religion of Tomorrow* (2017, Shambhala Publications).

[13] https://www.bbc.co.uk/religion/galleries/bhavachakra/
https://www.frontiersin.org/journals/psychology/articles/10.3389/fpsyg.2024.1293943/full;
https://pmc.ncbi.nlm.nih.gov/articles/PMC8694651/;
https://www.berkeleywellbeing.com/flourishing.html

[14] https://positivepsychology.com/positive-psychology-theory/

[15] https://www.nonsymbolic.org/finders/

[16] Christians might describe *nirvana* as that kind of peace. The Apostle Paul speaks of it in his Letter to the Philippians, 4:7. Hinduism speaks of *Brahman* and Islam of *Sakinah* – all of which include a profound sense of inner calm and equanimity, but in radically different interpretive frameworks.

[17] Photo by Alexander Caddy in 1896, now in the public domain Ghandara, ca. 3rd Century CE
https://en.m.wikipedia.org/wiki/File:Birth_of_buddha_peshawar.JPG

[18] *Lion's Roar*, July 13, 2021 (https://www.lionsroar.com/who-was-the-buddha)

[19] See "Miracles of Gautama Buddha" in *Wikipedia*

[20] Asita's Prediction. 3rd/4th century CE, Gandhara. From a photograph in the public domain. https://www.dhammawiki.com/index.php?title=File:Asita1.jpg

[21] *Sukhamala Sutta* (Discourse on Refinement), paraphrased

[22] Three of the Four Sights. Contemporary painting, © Hartmann Linge, Wikimedia Commons, CC-by-sa 3.0 https://commons.wikimedia.org/wiki/File:201304061243a_Wat_Bang_Riang.jpg

[23] https://en.wikipedia.org/wiki/Sramana. See also https://www.wisdomlib.org/definition/shramana#buddhism

[24] The exact meaning of Rahula's name is not clear to every scholar. But see https://buddhism.stackexchange.com/questions/3731/what-is-the-meaning-of-rahula and https://en.wikipedia.org/wiki/R%C4%81hula

[25] Relief Showing Prince Siddhartha's Great Departure Gandhara, 160-200 CE. Museum of Art and Archaeology, University of Missouri. https://maacollections.missouri.edu/ArgusNET/Portal.aspx?lang=en-US

[26] *Ariyapariyesana Sutta* (The Noble Search), translated by Thanissaro Bhikkhu.
https://www.accesstoinsight.org/tipitaka/mn/mn.026.than.html

[27] Gotama after years of austerity. Statue in Mahabodhi Temple.
From a photograph in the public domain
https://www.flickr.com/photos/90664717@N00/38669388120

[28] Sujata offers Rice Balls to Gotama. Photo Dharma from Sadao Thailand.
https://creativecommons.org/licenses/by/2.0
https://commons.wikimedia.org/wiki/File:085_Sujata_offers_Rice_(9189374231).jpg

[29] Gotama's Breakthrough. 10th Century CE Bihar, India. San Diego Museum of Art.
https://collection.sdmart.org/Media/images/1951-1960_Embark_Object_Photos/1960.58.jpg

[30] The *Sutta* "To Mahanama" contains a dialogue between the Buddha and Mahanama.

[31] Albert Einstein, written statement (September 1937), p. 70. Quoted by Tom McFarlane:
https://www.quora.com/What-are-Einsteins-views-on-Buddha

[32] *Dona Sutta* (To Dona)

[33] *Ayacana Sutta* (The Request)

[34] *Ayacana Sutta* (The Request)

[35] Sangharakshita's phrase

[36] This saying, revived in our time by Bruce Lee, is from the Chan/Zen tradition found in the *Shurangama Sutra*.

[37] Gold coin from Tillia Tepe, Ca. 100 BCE. Kabal Museum. https://commons.wikimedia.org/wiki/File:Tilia_Tepe_gold_token._Kabub_Museum.jpg

[38] See the *Nagara Sutta* (The City)

[39] *Tittha Sutta* (Belief)

[40] Blind men examining an elephant. Hanabusa Itchō (1652–1724), Japan. The image is in the public domain. https://en.wikipedia.org/wiki/File:Blind_monks_examining_an_elephant.jpg

[41] *Bahiya Sutta* (With Bahiya), paraphrased

[42] The Aged Buddha. From a Contemporary Mongolian Tanga - Source unknown.

[43] *Mahaparinibbana Sutta* (The Passing of the Buddha), paraphrased

[44] *Mahaparinibbana Sutta* (The Passing of the Buddha), paraphrased

[45] *Mahaparinibbana Sutta* (The Passing of the Buddha), translated by Sister Vajira & Francis Story

[46] *Mahaparinibbana Sutta* (The Passing of the Buddha), paraphrased

[47] *Mahaparinibbana Sutta* (The Passing of the Buddha), paraphrased

⁴⁸ Ananda weeping at the Buddha's death. East Javanese relief.
https://www.wikiwand.com/en/articles/Ananda#/media/File:039_Ananda_(25595327227).jpg

⁴⁹ *Mahaparinibbana Sutta* (The Passing of the Buddha), translated by Sister Vajira & Francis Story

⁵⁰ The First Council. By permission of the International Buddhist Society.
https://buddhisttemple.ca/buddhism/timeline/

⁵¹ https://encyclopediaofbuddhism.org/wiki/Śāsana

⁵² The Deer Park Instruction. From the Peace Pagoda at Willen Lake, Milton Keynes. Source: unknown
See https://www.theparkstrust.com/our-work/heritage/peace-pagoda/

⁵³ https://www.sokaglobal.org/resources/study-materials/buddhist-concepts/the-middle-way.html#:

⁵⁴ https://www.middlewaysociety.org/

⁵⁵ https://www.middlewaysociety.org/middle-way-philosophy/middle-way-philosophy-a-quick-guide/

⁵⁶ *Mahaparinibbana Sutta* (The Last Days of the Buddha), Section II, Verse 125

⁵⁷ *Dhammacakkappavattana Sutta* (The First Turning of the Dharma Wheel), author's paraphrase

⁵⁸ *Dhammacakkappavattana Sutta* (The First Turning of the Dharma Wheel), author's paraphrase

59 The Tian Tan "Big Buddha". Po Lin Monastery, Hong Kong. The photo is in the public domain. http://www.buddhistsymbols.org/assets/images/tian-tan-buddha-958765-1920-1076x717.jpg

60 What the Buddha Taught (1959, One World Publications), page 17

61 https://vinaire.me/2023/02/19/buddhism-the-four-noble-truths/

62 *Dhammacakkappavattana Sutta* (The First Turning of the Dharma Wheel), author's paraphrase

63 See "Ignorance vs Delusion - What's the difference?" in https://wikidiff.com/

64 https://medium.com/optim/how-a-fake-buddha-quote-completely-changed-my-life-for-the-better-2108ef8d07e6

65 *Dhammacakkappavattana Sutta*: Setting the Wheel of Dhamma in Motion, translation of Thanissaro Bhikkhu https://www.accesstoinsight.org/tipitaka/sn/sn56/sn56.011.than.html

66 https://secularbuddhistnetwork.org/the-core-concept-of-secular-buddhism-a-fourfold-task/

67 Peter Harvey, from his notes on the *Dhammacakkappavattana Sutta*

68 Bob Wilson developed his 12 Step Programme in the early years of Alcoholics Anonymous, which he founded with Bob Smith in 1935. For many thousands of suffering

individuals, this approach has proved a way out of a variety of addictions.

[69] *Dhammacakkappavattana Sutta* (The First Turning of the Dharma Wheel), author's paraphrase

[70] City of 10,000 Buddhas - The Wonderful Dharma Lotus Flower Sutra with Commentary Introduction 1

[71] *Mahaparinibbana Sutta* (Last Days of the Buddha*)*, III:7, author's paraphrase

[72] Buddha Head, with "Third (wisdom) Eye". Northwest India, 1-3 Century CE. Rhode Island School of Design. © Ad Meskens / Wikimedia Commons (permission to use freely).

[73] https://www.youtube.com/watch?v=s4uajFzgXSY

[74] From "Wisdom and Compassion", https://www.buddhanet.net/e-learning/qanda07

[75] https://www.wisdomlib.org/definition/samma#pali

[76] https://en.wikipedia.org/wiki/Praj%C3%B1%C4%81_(Buddhism)

[77] See the *Ariyapariyesana Sutta* (The Noble Search) and the *Maha-Saccaka Sutta* (The Longer Discourse to Saccaka)

[78] See https://www.lionsroar.com/5-practices-for-nurturing-happiness/

[79] Vishen Lakhiani, *The Code of the Extraordinary Mind: 10 Unconventional Laws to Redefine Your Life and Succeed on Your Own Terms* (Kindle Books, 2016)

[80] "The Kingdom of Heaven is Within You" is a phrase from the Bible, *Luke* 17:21, in which Jesus responds to a question about when the Kingdom of God will come.

[81] *Mahasaccaka Sutta* (The Greater Discourse with Saccaka), author's paraphrase – omitting the mention of rebirth which appears in the original.

[82] https://en.wikipedia.org/wiki/Fetter_(Buddhism)

[83] For example, "On the Construction of a Theory of Everything Based on Buddhist Cosmological Model" by Weicheng Cui and Linlin Kang (On the Construction of a Theory of Everything Based on Buddhist Cosmological Model (juniperpublishers.com) and https://www.jamyangnorbu.com/blog/2019/09/01/buddhas-theory-of-everything/

[84] *Assutava Sutta* (Uninstructed)

[85] Herbert Spencer, *The Study of Sociology*, Chapter II (1873)

[86] Blake wrote this poem in 1803, but it was not published until 1863.

[87] See, https://en.wikipedia.org/wiki/Spiritual_evolution, Ken Wilbur: *Sex, Ecology, Spirituality; The Spirit of Evolution,* 2nd Edition (2000, Shambala Publications) and Ken Wilbur: *Up from Eden; A Transpersonal View of Evolution* (2005, Pilgrim Publishing)

[88] https://www.rcpsych.ac.uk/docs/default-source/members/sigs/spirituality-spsig/what-is-spirituality-maya-spencer-x.pdf?sfvrsn=f28df052_2

[89] The Shakyamuni Daibutsu Bronze, ca. 609 CE, Nara, Japan.
Author: Chris 73.
https://commons.wikimedia.org/wiki/File:Asuka_dera_daibutsu.jpg

[90] https://louisethompson.com/intentions-vs-resolutions/

[91] https://www.betterup.com/blog/characteristics-of-a-determined-person/

[92] "On Right Intention", Buddhist Door Global Newsletter, August 2, 2021: https://www.buddhistdoor.net/features/on-right-intention/

[93] https://www.wisdomlib.org/definition/sankappa

[94] Matthew 6:25, which links this concept to an attachment to Jesus. Gautama sought no equivalent attachment (and some would argue, neither did the historical Jesus).

[95] *Magga-vibhanga Sutta*: "An Analysis of the Path", author's paraphrase

[96] https://seaoceaninfo.com/the-starfish-story-changing-lives-one-starfish-at-a-time/ and https://successminded.co/the-starfish-story-how-small-acts-make-a-big-difference/

[97] Ajahn Sucitto, *The Graduated Path*, Amaravati Publications, 2016. The punctuation has been changed from the original, for clarity.

[98] "A Theory of Human Motivation" by A. H. Maslow (1943) was initially published in *Psychological Review*, 50, 370-396

[99] Maslow, "Various meanings of transcendence", *Journal of Transpersonal Psychology:* 1, 56–66 (1969)

[100] Many Helping Hands of Kannon (Quan Yin). Japanese temple (unidentified location). Source Marvin Fry. https://uk.pinterest.com/pin/644648134148138206/

[101] Unitarian Clergyman and Signatory of the Humanist Manifesto (1933)

[102] https://sevenpillarsinstitute.org/glossary/buddhist-ethics/

[103] Joseph Fletcher popularised this perspective in *Situation Ethics: The New Morality* (1997)

[104] Ethics, John Dewey and James H. Tufts: Ethics (1922)

[105] https://www.irishtimes.com/culture/books/the-single-biggest-problem-in-communication-is-the-illusion-that-it-has-taken-place-1.4404586

[106] https://tricycle.org/article/nonviolent-communication-buddhism/

[107] *Cunda Kammaraputta Sutta* (A Dialogue with Cunda the Silversmith)

[108] See Paul Fleischman's "The Buddha Taught Nonviolence, not Pacifism" https://www.buddhistinquiry.org/article/the-buddha-taught-nonviolence-not-pacifism/#:~:text=Though%20it%20emphasizes%20nonvi

olence%2C%20it,life%20embedded%20in%20meditative%20insight

And John Cianciosi: "The Buddha Was Not a Vegetarian" https://www.theosophical.org/publications/quest-magazine/2901

[109] Meditating Buddha from a Rock-cut Stupa. Bojjana Konda, India. Photograph by Jvsnkk, 2012. https://www.flickr.com/photos/28772513@N07/8575201365/in/photostream/.

[110] *Kusala Sutta;* author's paraphrase

[111] https://www.quora.com/What-is-the-difference-between-right-action-and-right-effort-in-the-eightfold-path

[112] https://en.wikipedia.org/wiki/Manas_(early_Buddhism)

[113] See Napoleon Hill's *Golden Rules* (Wiley Publishing, 2008), Chapter Nine.

[114] *Sona Sutta* (About Sona), author's paraphrase

[115] *Samvara Sutta* (Book of Fours), *Sutta* 14. A modified version of Bhikkhu Bodhi's translation

[116] *Magga-vibhanga Sutta* (An Analysis of the Path)

[117] The *Visuddhimagga* (The Path of Purity) was translated by Bhikkhu Nanamoli and published in 1956 by the Buddhist Publication Society in Kandy, Sri Lanka

[118] See https://mindworks.org/blog/the-buddhist-concept-of-near-enemies/

[119] Spring Buddha. Source unknown

[120] Original quote by Ajahn Chah cited by his student, Jack Kornfield: https://jackkornfield.com/finding-the-middle-way/

[121] https://www.londonmindful.com/blog/mindfulness-misconceptions/

[122] https://www.lionsroar.com/the-eightfold-path-right-concentration/

[123] Found in both *Ambalatthikarahulovada Sutta* (Advice to Rahula at Ambalatthika)`and the *Magga-vibhanga Sutta* (An Analysis of the Path)

[124] "The Neuroscience of Mindfulness Meditation" (January 2017). https://www.researchgate.net/publication/319015377_The_Neuroscience_of_Mindfulness_Meditation/

[125] Experience Life Magazine; Deed - Attribution 3.0 Unported - Creative Commons

[126] https://www.londonmindful.com/blog/mindfulness-misconceptions/

[127] "Buddhism: A Method of Mind Training", 1994: https://www.accesstoinsight.org/lib/authors/bullen/bl042.html#:~:text=Buddhism%20is%20a%20way%20of,of%20suffering%20in%20everyday%20life

[128] See, for example, *Four Ways to Click: Rewire Your Brain for Stronger, More Rewarding Relationships* by Dr. Amy Banks (Penguin Publishing Group, 2015) and Lucy Jewel's "Neurorhetoric, Race, and the Law: Toxic Neural

Pathways and Healing Alternatives" in the Maryland Law Review, Volume 76 (2017)

[129] An Awakened Celt, Stucco figure, 2nd Century, CE *From Tapa-Kalan Monastery in Hadda,* Aghanistan. https://balkancelts.wordpress.com/2020/02/01/the-celtic-buddha-stucco-portrait-of-an-enlightened-celt-from-the-greco-buddhist-monastic-complex-at-hadda-in-eastern-afghanistan/

[130] 1990, HarperCollins Publishers

[131] Csikszentmihalyi's book was retitled *Flow: The Psychology of Happiness* in the Penguin Edition, 2002

[132] https://www.researchgate.net/publication/325273409_The_Neuroscience_of_Flow

[133] Meditating Buddha. Copy of 5th century CE original from Taxila Monastery, Taxila Museum, Pakistan. Creative Commons Licence 4.0. https://commons.wikimedia.org/w/index.php?curid=45797871

[134] https://www.trekstock.com/news/world-meditation-day-2023?gclid=EAIaIQobChMIuofct9GMgwMVHpJQBh0kgAvpEAAYASAAEgIf8PD_BwE

[135] *Pathama Assutavantu Sutta* (The Spiritually Unlearned)

[136] See https://historytheinterestingbits.com/2020/04/05/julian-of-norwich-all-shall-be-well/

¹³⁷ A paraphrase from the opening passages of *satipatthana*, (the Mindfulness of Breathing discourse)

¹³⁸ Lotus Flower. http://www.buddhistsymbols.org/lotusflowers.html

¹³⁹ https://healthypsych.com/learning-center-buddhist-psychology-theory-tools/

¹⁴⁰ https://link.springer.com/chapter/10.1007/978-3-031-10274-5_14

¹⁴¹ The process is referenced in "The Bundles" (*Kandha Sutta*) and many other discourses

¹⁴² *Anattalakkhana Sutta*, (The Discourse on the Not-Self Characteristic), Author's paraphrase

¹⁴³ For example, https://zenpsychiatry.com/the-three-buddhist-personality-types-which-one-are-you/ and https://www.idrlabs.com/buddhist-personality/test.php

¹⁴⁴ Jack Kornfield: *The Wise Heart* (Ryder Publishing, 2008); https://healthypsych.com/learning-center-buddhist-psychology-theory-tools/

¹⁴⁵ https://www.accesstoinsight.org/tipitaka/kn/khp/khp.5.nara.html#fn-2.16

¹⁴⁶ (*Prajnaparamitahridaya Sutra*) The Discourse on the Heart of the Perfection of Wisdom (author's paraphrase

¹⁴⁷ "Om ma ni pad me hum" Tibetan Mantra
Author: Christopher J. Fynn/Wikimedia Commons/CC BY-SA 3.0 & GFDL.
https://commons.wikimedia.org/wiki/File:Om-mani-

padme-hum_02.svg#/media/File:Om-mani-padme-hum_01.svg

[148] https://en.wikipedia.org/wiki/Om_mani_padme_hum#According_to_the_14th_Dalai_Lama

[149] https://www.researchgate.net/publication/292255944_The_Six_Perfections_Buddhism_and_the_Cultivation_of_Character

[150] *The Six Perfections: Buddhism & the Cultivation of Character* (Oxford University Press, 2011), page 3

[151] *What Colour Is a Conservative? My Life and My Politics* (Zondervan Press, 2003)

[152] Dalai Lama Quotes. (n.d.). BrainyQuote.com. Retrieved March 12, 2025, from BrainyQuote.com Web site: https://www.brainyquote.com/quotes/dalai_lama_108820

[153] Ascribed to a variety of sources, from Lao Tzu (Sixth Century BCE) to Frank Outlaw (Twentieth Century). https://quote investigator.com/2013/01/10/watch-your-thoughts/

[154] Gabrielle Giffords. *Gabby: A Story of Courage and Hope* (Simon and Schuster, 2011), derived from Zig Zigler's version; for example, *See You at the Top* (Nightengale-Conant, 1989).

[155] Published as a Portfolio Penguin Book, September 2019. This book quickly became a New York Times #1 bestseller.

[156] https://www.ucl.ac.uk/news/2009/aug/how-long-does-it-take-form-habit

[157] https://www.learnreligions.com/maha-pajapati-and-the-first-nuns-449897

[158] See "Buddhism and Caste System" by Y. Krishan, *East and West:* Vol. 48, No. 1/2 (June 1998), pp. 41-55

[159] An expression of the Apostle Paul in *Romans* 12:15

[160] Two of the four seated Buddhas in the Kyaik Pun Photo by Hans A. Rosbach. Creative Commons licence 3.0 Unported license. File: Kyaik Pun Paya - Bago, Myanmar 20130219-01.jpg - Wikimedia Commons
Buddhist iconography often depicts four Buddha faces looking in many directions, thus aware of the needs of every being. These four faces can represent the Immeasurables (*appamanna*) or "heavenly abodes" / "sublime attitudes" (*brahma vihara*). Each of these aspects of love begins inwardly, with thoughts and emotions, with a natural inclination for an outward and active orientation.

[161] https://www.renown-travel.com/burma/bago/kyaikpunpagoda.html

[162] *Upaḍḍha Sutta (*Half the Spiritual Life)

[163] Buddha, Odilon Redon, 1904. Museum d'Orsay, Paris Gryiffindor, Public Domain. https://commons.wikimedia.org/wiki/File:Redon.bouddha.jpg

[164] https://www.accesstoinsight.org/lib/authors/thanissaro/refuge.html/

[165] https://www.docsity.com/en/the-three-refuges-background-information/8926710/

[166] *A Guide to the Buddhist Path* (1997)

[167] Thanissaro Bhikkhu: "Going for Rge" (*Insight Journal*, Spring 1996)

[168] The author's paraphrase of a section of the *Garava Sutta* (Reverence)

[169] Vinaya, Mahāvibhaṅga 1:4 (Cited in *The Life of the Buddha* by Bhikkhu Nanamoli (Buddhist Publication Society, 2001)

[170] https://ancient-buddhist-texts.net/English-Texts/Great-Chronicles/12.htm

[171] Nanamoli, *The Life of the Buddha*, page 49

[172] See, for example, the *Vera Sutta* (Discourse on Animosity) and the *Sammādiṭṭhi Sutta* (Right View)

[173] *Dhammapada*, verses 190-192

[174] Photo and quote: "Seeking Refuge -Ahed" by Kitty Gale, 2021. https://kittygale.co.uk/personal/seeking-refuge

[175] *Bodhisattva* Ksitigarbha ("Earth Store"). Who vowed to postpone his full Awakening until all beings were released from hell.
http://www.buddhistsymbols.org/buddhaimages.html

[176] https://suttacentral.net/ma6/en/patton?lang=en&layout=plain&reference=none&notes=asterisk&highlight=false&script=latin

[177] See the essay "No-self or Not-self?" by Thanissaro Bhikkhu (Access to Insight website, 1996): https://www.accesstoinsight.org/lib/authors/thanissaro/notself2.html

[178] The *Bodhicaryavatara*, "On the Perfection of Forbearance", verses 3-6

[179] Jung wrote an essay, "Instinct and the Unconscious" which introduced the term and concept. https://bpspsychub.onlinelibrary.wiley.com/doi/10.1111/j.2044-8295.1919.tb00003

[180] *Bodhisattva* Ksitigarbha ("Earth Store"). Who vowed to postpone his full Awakening until all beings were released from hell. http://www.buddhistsymbols.org/buddhaimages.html

[181] https://psychologily.com/power-of-altruism/#Why_is_Altruism_Important

[182] Such as Ralf Waldo Emerson, Samuel Smiles, and Napoleon Hill

[183] https://quotes.guide/tony-robbins/quote/the-secret-of-living-is-giving/ See also, https://simplyputpsych.co.uk/psych-101-1/what-is-altruism-a-psychological-perspective

184 See, for example, https://pmc.ncbi.nlm.nih.gov/articles/PMC10326385/ and https://socialsci.libretexts.org/Bookshelves/Psychology/Social_Psychology_and_Personality/Principles_of_Social_Psychology_1e_International_Edition/08%3A_Helping_and_Altruism/8.01%3A_Understanding_Altruism_-_Self_and_Other_Concerns

185 See *Philosophy of Ecology* by Kevin de Laplante and others (2011)

186 Listen to Dave Davies interview with Forestry Professor Suzanne Simard about her memoir, *Finding the Mother Tree* (https://www.npr.org/sections/health-shots/2021/05/04/993430007/trees-talk-to-each-other-mother-tree-ecologist-hears-lessons-for-people-too).

187 Available from tonyrobbins.com

188 Thich Nhat Hanh, Creating True Peace: Ending Violence in Yourself, Your Family, Your Community, and the World (Free Press, 2003)

189 See "Mindfulness: A strategy for social engagement?" by Meg-John Barker(https://www.rewriting-the-rules.com/self/mindfulness-strategy-social-engagement/) and "Mindfulness in the Context of Engaged Buddhism: A Case for Engaged Mindfulness" by Brian D. Somers (https://www.mdpi.com/2077-1444/13/8/746)

190 https://banotes.org/india-earliest-times-300-ce/emperor-ashoka-war-remorse-dhamma-path/

[191] See, for example "The Path of Peace: Using the Buddhist 'Middle Way' to Encourage IHL Compliance - Religion and Humanitarian Principles" in blogs.icrc.org and "Why do Families Fight? Buddha's advice for Families on Resolving Conflicts" in buddhaweekly.com

[192] See https://www.oxfordbibliographies.com/display/document/obo-9780195393521/obo-9780195393521-0251.xml

[193] See "In Myanmar, Buddhist Monks Preach Nationalism" (www.foreignpolicy.com): "Buddhist Monks and the Politics of Lanka's Civil War" (www.equinoxpub.com); https://www.e-ir.info/2023/08/31/buddhist-nationalism-and-extremism-in-myanmar-and-north-america/; https://en.wikipedia.org/wiki/Sri_Lankan_Civil_War; and https://www.worldwatchmonitor.org/2016/10/peaceful-buddhisms-violent-face-in-sri-lanka/

[194] "Buddhist Nationalism and Extremism in Myanmar and North America by Brenna Artinger", E-International Relations website, 31 August 2023. https://www.e-ir.info/2023/08/31/buddhist-nationalism-and-extremism-in-myanmar-and-north-america/

[195] Two Wolves, Photo by Raed Mansour. https://creativecommons.org/license 2.0/ https://commons.wikimedia.org/wiki/File:Niko_and_Sparrow,_Gray_Wolves,_Wolf_Park_(51095976734).jpg

[196] Darrin Drda: *The Four Global Truths; Awakening to the Peril and Promise of Our Times* (2011, Evolver Editions, Berkeley, California).

[197] https://www.bbc.co.uk/religion/galleries/bhavachakra/ This Incredible Buddhist Mandala Depicts the Insanity of American Life

[198] Darrin Drda: *The Four Global Truths; Awakening to the Peril and Promise of Our Times* (2011, Evolver Editions, Berkeley, California), p. 270

[199] From Plantfifty Instagram site (@plantfifty)

[200] "The Encyclopaedia Britannica describes a mandala as representing an "area that serves as a receptacle for the gods and as a collection point of universal forces. Man (the microcosm), by mentally "entering" the mandala and "proceeding" toward its centre, is by analogy guided through the cosmic processes of disintegration and reintegration." (https://www.britannica.com/topic/mandala-diagram)

[201] A finger pointing to the moon, from a Tibetan Wheel of Life. https://creativecommons.org/licenses/by-sa/3.0/ https://www.mountainsoftravelphotos.com/Tibet%20-%20Buddhism/Wheel%20Of%20Life/Wheel%20Of%20Life/slides/Tibetan%20Buddhism%20Wheel%20Of%20Life%2001%20Buddha%20Upper%20Right.jpg

[202] "In the psychology of human behaviour, denialism is a person's choice to deny reality as a way to avoid a psychologically uncomfortable truth."

https://www.linkedin.com/pulse/dangerous-impact-denial-tian-dayton-phd

[203] Wheel of Life: Inner Circles, from travel2photograph.com: https://travel2photograph.wordpress.com/2011/02/15/buddhism-the-tibetan-wheel-of-life/

[204] From A *Commentary on Great Perfection*, section 3C, translated from the Tibetan (https://www.wisdomlib.org/buddhism/book/the-great-chariot/d/doc212800.html)

[205] https://www.nichirenlibrary.org/en/dic/Content/T/291#:~:text=The%20Sanskrit%20word%20nid%C4%81na%20means,that%20leads%20to%20the%20next

[206] See both https://en.wikipedia.org/wiki/Bhavacakra and https://en.wikipedia.org/wiki/Early_Christian_art_and_architecture

[207] "The Yoga of Narcissism" published in the Elephant Journal (https://www.elephantjournal.com/2013/03/the-yoga-of-narcissism-darrin-drda/)

[208] Darrin Drda, The Four Global Truths (2011) is published by Evolver Editions, Berkeley, California

[209] See John 17: 14-15 and Revelation 21:1

[210] "Veneration of the Three Jewels", 2nd Century CE, Gandhara. The Ethnological Museum in Berlin. Photo by Daderot. Creative Commons CC0 1.0 Universal Public Domain. https://commons.wikimedia.org/wiki/File:Veneration_of_t

he_Three_Jewels,_Chorasan,_Gandhara,_2nd_century_AD,_schist_-_Ethnological_Museum,_Berlin_-_DSC01642.jpg

[211] https://www.youtube.com/watch?v=F2RousymNt0

[212] The Herald Newspaper (Scotland), 22 May 2024

[213] Jack Kornfield: *The Wise Heart: A Guide to the Universal Teachings of Buddhist Psychology* (2009), Bantam Press, New York

[214] See https://www.goodreads.com/quotes/501883-the-religion-of-the-future-will-be-a-cosmic-religion/ which admits "no source.

[215] https://www.bbc.co.uk/future/article/20150727-what-are-the-limits-of-human-vision

[216] "Perception Is Not Reality" | Psychology Today blog, 5 August 2019. https://www.psychologytoday.com/us/blog/the-power-prime/201908/perception-is-not-reality?msockid=1d40170cc369678a041802a1c2896638

[217] https://www.stewardship.org.uk/blogs/jesus-good-steward

[218] See, for example, the Christian Aid, Tear Fund, and Caritas websites.

[219] https://en.wikipedia.org/wiki/Dalit

[220] https://www.marxists.org/archive/ambedkar/writings-and-speeches/Volume_05.pdf

[221] Bhimrao Ramji "Ambedkar and the Great Conversion" - Tricycle

[222] https://www.vocabulary.com/dictionary/transcendence

[223] For other Buddhist prayers, see https://www.xavier.edu/jesuitresource/online-resources/prayer-index/buddhist-prayers

[224] https://slate.com/culture/2003/02/why-i-ditched-buddhism.html

[225] Stephen Batchelor: *Secular Buddhism; Imagining the Dharma in an Uncertain World* 2017; Yale University Press)

[226] https://www.britannica.com/topic/agnosticism

[227] One of the earliest seated Buddha Icons. 1st to 2nd century Gandhara, Bronze with traces of gold leaf. The Metropolitan Museum of Art. https://www.facebook.com/photo.php?fbid=10151771954511675&set=a.212955701674.174468.196174216674&type=1&relevant_count=1

[228] *Lotus in a Stream; Essays in Basic Buddhism*: 2000, Weatherhill

[229] https://www.youtube.com/watch?v=hnlUkccRDrk

[230] Ecclesiastes 3:1

[231] From paintings of Life of Gautama Buddha - AsalhaPuja.jpg. https://creativecommons.org/licenses/by-sa/3.0/

Printed in Dunstable, United Kingdom